English
Eccentrics
and
Their Bizarre
Behaviour

English Eccentrics and Their Bizarre Behaviour

David Long

With illustrations by Les Evans

REMEMBER WHEN

First published in Great Britain in 2009 by
REMEMBER WHEN
An imprint of
Pen & Sword Books Ltd
47 Church Street
Barnsley
South Yorkshire
S70 2AS

ISBN 978 1 84468 055 9

Typeset by Phoenix Typesetting, Auldgirth, Dumfriesshire
Printed and bound by CPI UK

Pen & Sword Books Ltd incorporates the Imprints of Pen & Sword Aviation,
Pen & Sword Maritime, Pen & Sword Military, Wharncliffe Local History,
Pen & Sword Select, Pen & Sword Military Classics, Leo Cooper, Remember When,
Seaforth Publishing and Frontline Publishing.

For a complete list of Pen & Sword titles please contact
PEN & SWORD BOOKS LIMITED
47 Church Street, Barnsley, South Yorkshire, S70 2AS, England
E-mail: enquiries@pen-and-sword.co.uk
Website: www.pen-and-sword.co.uk

Contents

Fantasy abandoned by reason produces impossible monsters
Francisco Goya (1746-1828)

Introduction

CONSIDERATE FELLOW that he was, Lord Berners finished building a 140-ft folly in 1935 and put up a sign warning that anyone committing suicide by leaping from the top did so at his own risk. James Burnett, a senior Eighteenth Century judge sitting as Lord Monboddo, believed that men were born with tails – a fact he said was concealed by a conspiracy of midwives who cut them all off at birth. Sir Francis Galton, using a system only he could understand, spent years compiling a map of the country showing where the most beautiful and the very ugliest women could be found. And in 1976, a former schoolmaster called Ernest Digweed who was confident of the second coming, left £26,000 which the Public Trustee 'upon obtaining proof which shall satisfy them of His identity, shall pay to Lord Jesus Christ'.

Ostentatious or absurdly secretive, over-ambitious, daft or just utterly, utterly hopeless, eccentrics are loved by the English – which have a special fondness for their own. To us they are characters not crackpots, potty but in a good way (rather than merely mad) and whilst we might, if pressed to do so, grudgingly acknowledge that other countries produce eccentrics of their own – the French motor-car manufacturer Ettore Bugatti, for example, who insisted on special shoes being made with separate compartments for his big toes – theirs we tend to think somewhat silly, whereas our own we celebrate as the very spirit of our isles' character and individuality.

In part this is because there is nothing more boring than being ordinary; but another reason we like them so much is that the best of them are multi-faceted rather than being simply obsessive or monomaniacs whose habits were allowed to get out of hand. The aforementioned 14th Baron Berners, for example, was also a diplomat, a painter and a noted composer of ballet scores and opera. Sir Francis Galton, besides being an exceptionally well-educated cousin of Charles Darwin's, was the first man to explain the complexities of anticyclones and later went on to fund his own academic chair at London University. And 'Mad Jack' Fuller was a popular and

ECCENTRIC ENGLISH CUSTOMS

- Did you know that each spring, ignoring modernising dictats from the Eurocrats and standing at makeshift pulpit aboard a lifeboat, the vicar of Hastings traditionally blesses the sea which divides us? Or that along the coast at Rye the locals celebrate May Day by throwing hot pennies into the drink?
- The most elaborate spring ritual is that held at Dunmow, namely the famous Flitch Trials which have been held in the pretty little Essex town for the last 900 years. In these mock-judicial proceedings, complete with wigs and gowns and with a flitch or side of bacon for the winners, married couples in the parish try to convince a jury of six maids and six bachelors that they have neither been unfaithful nor exchanged a single cross word.
- Unsurprisingly the historic City of London is rich with such quirky behaviour too – for example the annual Swan-Upping Ceremony on the Thames which sees liveried members of the Vintners Company nicking the birds' beaks to show whether they belong to the Queen or to the Company. Then there is the Doggett's Coats and Badge Race in which, every August since 1721, newly-qualified Thames Watermen race from London Bridge to Chelsea in the hope of winning the princely sum of a fiver, a scarlet coat, some breeches, a pair of shoes and an enormous silver badge.
- Similarly on Christmas Day in Hyde Park, swimmers compete on the chilly Serpentine for the Peter Pan Cup, inaugurated by Sir J.M. Barrie in 1864 and which sometimes requires the competitors to break the ice first.
- The High Almoner, traditionally a senior bishop, still wears a towel at his waist as a reminder to Christian kings to follow the example of Christ and to echo His humility in washing the feet of others at the Last Supper. (Elizabeth I was a great fan of this, but concerns over the generally low standard of hygiene displayed by the masses meant that actual foot-washing came to an end with a more fastidious King George I in 1730.)
- Barges no longer provide the quickest way to travel from the palace at Hampton Court to Westminster or to Greenwich – although the way things are going with traffic in London that could change – but when the Crown Jewels travel by carriage they traditionally do so in the company of the Queen's Barge Master and her Royal Watermen.

well-regarded Parliamentarian even if these days he is remembered (if at all) for building a 40-ft steeple in a field after realising that he'd made a mistake wagering a friend that he could see the village church from his dining room window.

Among eccentrics, builders such as Fuller and Berners are perhaps the best known, probably because they leave behind such concrete evidence of their exploits. But eccentricity can take many other forms as well – although these days most observers recognise that to be a real eccentric requires more than just a single isolated act, however loony the act appears; Gordon East and Julie Fillipeto marrying each other in a lion's cage, for example, or Chris and Sue Glazier from Kent who spent their wedding night driving round the M25 in a luxury coach equipped with a suitably well-appointed honeymoon suite.

The real heroes of this book (and they're mostly English, although the Scots, Irish and Welsh do get a look-in along the way) demonstrate a lifetime's commitment to the cause of being definitely, decidedly and irredeemably odd.

These include chaps such as Lt. Colonel Alfred D. Wintle, who sincerely held the belief that time spent anywhere but on the back of a horse was time wasted. Sir George Reresby Sitwell, who banned electricity from his household until well into the 1940s, tried to pay for his son's Eton College education with pigs and potatoes, and attempted to stencil Chinese willow patterns on his herd of cows. A favourite of the author's, William Buckland,

Oxford's first Professor of Geology, famously claimed – and was able to demonstrate – that he could tell wherever he was in the country simply by tasting the local topsoil.

This book is dedicated to them and to others like them – and to my children Hugo and Ivo in the heartfelt hope that they don't end up the same way.

CHAPTER ONE

Builders

⟹⟐⟸

GERALD HUGH TYRWHITT-WILSON (1883–1950)

Monochrome meals and a towering genius

MAINTAINING the aristocracy's record of rampant eccentricity until well into the Twentieth Century, the 14th Baron Berners knowingly invited a horse to afternoon tea. Called Moti, it was owned by the future Lady Betjeman, the poet laureate's wife, and was photographed taking tea from her saucer. The Baron famously dyed the pigeons at his Oxfordshire home a variety of bright colours, taking care to use a dye that did them no harm. He did have an occasional penchant for monochromatic meals, but his fellow composer Stravinsky reported that, 'If his mood was pink, lunch might consist of beet soup, lobster, tomatoes and strawberries.' (Berners would have his unfortunate birds carefully re-dyed to match what he was eating when the need arose.) His lordship also went to the trouble of having a piano keyboard installed in the back of his Rolls-Royce, in order that his music could accompany him wherever he went. A lifelong bachelor, he equipped his whippets with diamond-studded collars.

Despite such exertions on his part – not to mention a busy professional life as a diplomat, composer and writer – it was Berners' passion for building which really put him on the map, particularly when a distant but vociferous neighbour objected at length to his plans to build an isolated 140-ft folly tower of his own design on a corner of his Farringdon estate.

The gentleman in question, a certain Admiral Clifton-Browne, objected to it on the grounds that the proposed tower would spoil the view from his own house. When Berners, conducting his own defence, suggested that Clifton-Browne would be able to see his tower only with the aid of a

telescope, the old sea-dog indignantly pointed out that being a retired admiral he naturally never looked at the world through anything else. Capt. Salty went to court to prove his point too, but in 1935 Berners finally won the day – despite defending his tower on the grounds that 'it will be entirely useless'. When his pride and joy was at last completed, he put up a sign warning that *Members Of The Public Committing Suicide From This Tower Do So At Their Own Risk.*

Around the estate he erected numerous equally idiosyncratic signs including some advising trespassers that stray dogs would be shot and that cats would be whipped. And whilst far from reclusive, he was known to go to very great lengths indeed to secure a private compartment when travelling by train.

Apparently his most successful ruse was dressing up with dark glasses and a black skullcap before leaning out of the window and beckoning passers-by to join him. If this didn't work – and presumably it did most of the time – he would pull a giant thermometer out of an inside pocket and, with an increasingly distressed expression on his face, proceed every few minutes to take his temperature. Understandably unnerved by the likely implications of his behaviour, most fellow travellers found somewhere else to sit pretty soon – which of course was his Lordship's intention all along.

WACKY TOWN PLANS WHICH NEVER QUITE MADE IT

- Many of the country's best-known landmarks were conceived to be quite different from how we see them today. It was originally proposed, for example, that Lord Nelson stand not at the top but at the foot of his column, as once he had stood before the mast. One of Wren's initial sketches for St Paul's Cathedral had a huge pineapple on top of the stately dome. (The exotic fruit was all the rage at the time, having just been introduced from the West Indies.) In 1918, the American shopping magnate Gordon Selfridge envisaged a square tower to crown his famous Oxford Street store that was so massive it would have caused the entire edifice to collapse under its weight.
- An Irish MP, Colonel (later Sir) Frederick Trench, spent decades lobbying for a number of completely barmy schemes including one to build a giant pyramid covering the whole of Trafalgar Square and another for an immense new royal palace. Approached along an avenue several hundred feet wide, and stretching from the City to Hyde Park, the latter would have required the demolition along the way of Covent Garden, the Crusaders' ancient Temple Church and much of the West End. Oddly enough the planners weren't having any of it.
- Equally, it could surely have been only fantasy for the Greater London Council in 1967 to consider running twin overhead passenger monorails to run down the middle of Regent Street. Or indeed for Charles Glover in 1931 to propose the construction of his novel King's Cross Aerodrome, a giant six-spoked wheel half a mile in diameter and balanced on top of the existing railway station. Glover's idea was for aircraft to land on the three runways made up by the six spokes, although what happened to them if they overshot hardly bears thinking about.
- Nor was the aforementioned Trench alone in having designs on the very Heart of Empire. John Goldicutt, having failed to oust Nelson's likeness from Trafalgar Square in favour of his own immense statue of William IV, proposed filling the

square with a replica Roman colosseum which rose four or five storeys high. Goldicutt claimed this vast eliptical warren would provide a suitably grand home for the Royal Academy as well as various learned societies of literature, science, astronomy and geology. Happily, and as he had at Trafalgar, Nelson prevailed and stands there still.

- In the 1880s, a chap called John Leighton seriously suggested redrawing the boundaries of every London borough so that each one would be hexagonal. The idea was to stop cabbies overcharging. A century earlier, a House of Commons Committee spent several days considering a barely credible plan to straighten the River Thames. This scheme's sponsor, one Willey Reveley, proposed to dig a new channel nearly a mile long in order to save ships wasting time sailing round the Isle of Dogs.

- And still on the river, that most respected engineer Robert Stephenson approved plans for the Thames Viaduct Railway, a giant latticework of steel enabling trains to run down the centre of the river. Then an architect called Harry Newton suggested building a pair of massive mid-stream islands there instead to accommodate new government offices, the central law courts and some private luxury apartments. He quickly abandoned the scheme, however, after being asked how much it would cost.

- Perhaps the most extraordinary scheme, however, if only because construction work on it actually began, was Wembley's copy of the Eiffel Tower. In 1891, the entrepreneur Sir Edward Watkin set out to 'out-Eiffel' the French on 280 acres of grassy north-west London he'd acquired expressly for this purpose. More than 100,000 people came to see the work in progress but the money soon ran out and for a dozen years or so the folly quietly rusted away, its scrap value estimated to be unequal to the cost of demolition. Eventually, in 1907, fewer than a dozen people turned up to see bolts of dynamite put beneath the tower's four steel legs and the whole ensemble blown to bits. By then Watkin was long dead and today Wembley Stadium occupies the site.

- Similarly barmy schemes continue to appear. As recently as 1959 another favourite spot came close to annihilation when a Birmingham developer actually managed to secure planning permission to plonk a vast, faceless 20-storey block right on top of Piccadilly Circus. Blank and almost windowless on the one side, his squat, square tower's only distinguishing feature was a 93-ft wide roof-top propeller – actually a revolving crane to be used for replacing the area's traditionally garish neon advertisements. Fortunately public opinion did for it in the end, though only after a long and bitter battle.

JOHN FULLER (1757–1834)

By a bet inspired

Down in East Sussex, 'Mad Jack' Fuller was a more prolific builder than Berners; a substantial larger-than-life Parliamentarian who despite being rudely described by the Speaker as 'an insignificant little fellow in a wig' (he actually weighed 22 st) and physically ejected from the House by the Serjeant-at-Arms, was later offered a peerage – although this was immediately declined. Today in Brightling, where the pub still bears his name and arms, he is best remembered for building a gigantic 40-ft steeple in a field simply to win a wager made with a group of friends.

An admirable three-bottles-a-day man, the port-drinking Fuller made the bet after one evening insisting that he could see the spire of St Giles at Dallington from his windows at Brightling Park. On discovering the following morning that he could not, he took prompt steps to remedy the situation – and thus to win the bet – by having a replica of the spire built on a spot where it could indeed be seen from his dining room.

As it happens, this was to be just one of many fairly eccentric erections thrown up to enliven the environs of Brightling Park. In times of high unemployment for example, Fuller, whilst personally somewhat impatient of beggars, was to spend a good part of his inheritance taking on local men and paying them to build for him. In return for his generosity, the men built mile after mile of handsome stone walls around his estate. Fuller's other public benefactions included paying for Eastbourne's first lifeboat, financing the building of the Belle Toute Lighthouse (at Beachy Head) and paying a hefty

3,000 guineas at auction for Bodiam Castle in order to save it from destruction.

Eventually becoming disillusioned with his political career, Fuller was to spend yet more of his fortune constructing buildings of the most inconsequential sort – which is to say, of course, follies of the purest and most perfect sort.

As a result, trippers today can still see his obelisk known as the Brightling Needle, its summit a full 646 ft above sea level, as well as a fine rotunda and a brick pillar topped by an iron flame, a cannon and an anchor (standing as a reminder of the foundries which which accounted for much of the Fuller family fortune).

Fuller also built himself a hermit's tower – a must-have, as such things were very much in keeping with the fashion of the time. However, when it was completed (and despite advertising for someone willing to live in it and to refrain from cutting his hair, beard and nails, or from speaking to any one for a period of not less than seven years) he failed to find anyone prepared to live in it.

With such a track record, it was perhaps inevitable that 'Mad Jack' would save the best until last and, after a good life, he chose to be buried at Brightling churchyard in a huge pyramid designed for him by Sir Robert Smirke, architect of the British Museum.

Sir Robert had earlier built an observatory for his client, but the pyramid is the finer piece, its purpose, said Fuller, being to prevent him being eaten by his own family. Without it, he explained whilst planning his final resting place, 'the worms will eat me, the ducks will eat the worms and my relatives will eat the ducks'. Instead, much like Charlemagne is reputed to be in his, 'Mad Jack' is in his mausoleum still, seated upright on an iron chair, carefully positioned before a table holding a roast chicken and a bottle of port and surrounded by broken glass 'so that when the devil comes for me he might at least cut his feet'.

GEORGE VILLIERS, DUKE OF BUCKINGHAM (1628–87)

Si monumentum requiris, circumspice

Clearly you don't have to be a duke to a have high opinion of yourself, but presumably if you're that way inclined anyway a senior rank is not going to help matters.

The examples are legion, but a favourite has to be George Villiers, 2nd Duke of Buckingham whose family in 1624 came into the possession of a generous, seven acre site besides the Thames in London. It had previously been owned by the bishops of Norwich, and his father the 1st Duke (also called George) had restored the bishops' old estate which at that time encompassed an incredible 50 houses, ten cottages, four stableblocks and seven interconnecting gardens. He also built a magnificent water gate which today is the sole survivor on the site, marooned and melancholy and now set back from the river in Embankment Gardens.

Following his murder in 1628, however, the place was only used intermittently until the 2nd Duke, heavily mortgaged (and realising that a number of speculators were greedily eyeing its potentially very valuable site) gave permission for the old palace to be torn down and the land developed. Of course at this time, it was not uncommon for landlords and developers to have streets and squares named after them, and indeed the practice continues today, most obviously in the way the fragile egos of time-serving local councillors are shored up using precisely the same method.

Not for the first time, however, Buckingham went a step further than most and having secured a useful £30,000 for the house and its gardens, insisted that the new network of streets and lanes being planned for the site by developer Nicholas Barbon record every fragment of his name and title. Thus today we have Buckingham Street, Villiers Street, Duke Street – now part of John Adam Street – and George Street, which was eventually to become York Buildings. Also for a while there was Of Alley, until this was eventually renamed York Place by another local councillor clearly lacking a sense of history – and humour.

CHARLES SEYMOUR, DUKE OF SOMERSET (1662–1748)

Eyes front!

According to those who knew him, the nickname given to Charles Seymour – aka 'The Proud Duke' – was already well deserved and upon marrying Elizabeth Percy in 1682 the 6th Duke clearly went over the edge.

The heiress to the ancient wealth and titles of the Earls of Northumberland, what Elizabeth brought to the marriage enabled His Grace to indulge not just his passion for pomp and ceremony, but also his now unshakeable belief that the lower orders were unfit even to look at him.

And unfortunately his own definition of what constituted the 'lower orders' seemed to include just about everyone, even his own children, one of whom having had the temerity to sit down in his presence promptly found herself deprived of a £20,000 inheritance (and this at Seventeeth Century values).

Little wonder then that the great unwashed were well beyond the pale, and that the Duke refused to talk to them or have any dealings with them beyond the occasional order which he issued using a form of sign language and gesture.

Unlike the reclusive 5th Duke of Portland, however (see later), Seymour's icy silence had nothing to do with his being shy and retiring. He was a snob, pure and simple, and one who went to some extraordinary lengths to avoid the lower classes, so offended was he by the idea that somebody ordinary might even glimpse his magnificence.

Most famously this included ordering the construction of a whole series of houses to be built along the routes running from his rural estates to London (in this way he always had somewhere private and clean to break his journey) and whilst he somehow got to grips with the notion of using the public highway like everyone else, he employed a number of outriders whose job it was to travel ahead of him and clear the route of commoners. Amazing.

JULIUS DREWE (1856-1931)

Retail magnate's dream

Apparently Sir Edward Coke (1552–1634) was the first to argue that an Englishman's house is his castle, and notwithstanding the fact that this former Chancellor was merely expressing a legal nicety, the reality is that deep down most of us probably wish it really was.

Not many genuine castles come onto the market these days, and of those that do – isolated, damp, virtually impossible to heat – most would be a complete and utter nightmare to own. Of course, given the wherewithal (The Lottery, Saturday night, 8pm, it could be you) one could always build a nice new one. On a somewhat modest scale, the architect John Taylor did just that, his Castle Gryn being completed in Wales in the late 1970s. But most these days accept that the last *real* modern castle is the National Trust's Castle Drogo in Devon, it having been designed for a department store millionaire back in the 1920s.

Drewe made his money as the founder-proprietor of the Home & Colonial Stores, and destined to lose his heir (his eldest son died at Ypres in the Great War), he retired at the age of 33 to spend the majority of that fortune building Castle Drogo. Today it still towers over the village of Drewsteignton, there being nothing accidental about the location, for by the time of his retirement the shopping magnate supposed he was a descendent of Drogo de Teign (who had come over with the Conqueror in 1066) and that Drewsteignton was where he'd had his fortress.

To help him along with this harmless if somewhat costly fantasy he engaged the services of Sir Edwin Lutyens in 1910, promising him the substantial sum of £50,000 (this at a time when the First Sea Lord earned just £1,500 annually at the Admiralty) in exchange for 'a medieval fortress to match the grandeur of the site' and doubtless too of his imaginative lineage.

Lutyens was a busy man, but began work immediately. Even so, Castle Drogo was not completed until 1931 for such was the scale of the enterprise. In the end, Mr Drewe had a mere eight weeks in which to enjoy his new home before he suffered a stroke and went to join his maker, his son Adrian and – who knows – maybe even Drogo de Teign as well.

His architect had been nothing if not thorough, however, building a full-scale replica of the castle in canvas and wood in order that his patron could get an idea of the finished article before work on the real thing actually began. When it did, the results quickly proved to be as majestic as hoped for and well matched to its moorland site some 900 ft above the village. It is also enormous, even though the extensive 20-year build period was sufficient to construct only a third of the walls, courtyards, barbican, gatehouse, great hall and great chamber which the two men had envisaged back in 1910.

Perhaps the most surprising thing about Drogo, however, is its purity. It's been likened to a prison, and even a biscuit box, but to his credit Drewe eschewed the usual Victorian or Edwardian approach to this kind of thing – the pursuit of the picturesque or the pastiche – and instead had Lutyens create a Twentieth Century version of the medieval ideal. To Drewe this meant no pitched roofs, no drainpipes and absolutely no central heating to warm its huge granite mass – although curiously he later specified more than 300 electric sockets and a very new-fangled vacuum-cleaning system which sucked the dust into vents set into the walls.

Today, as a result, it is forbidding to say the least, and certainly a long way from being the loveliest of the National Trust's many properties or, one supposes, the most comfortable in which to live. The views across the Teign and across Dartmoor are fantastic, and some of Lutyens' medieval detailing might raise a smile, but there's a certain severity to the place which even the somewhat idiosyncratic Spanish furnishings do little to alleviate

The fenestration doesn't help either, with great stretches of wall barely broken by the castle's tiny windows, and for the modern day visitor, particularly when numbers are low, the overwhelming sensation is one of endless stone corridors, chilly stone vaults, and a sense of seclusion. Still, a proper castle is what Mr Drewe ordered, and a proper castle is what he got.

WILLIAM BECKFORD (1759-1844)

Brought down by beer and bankruptcy

Of all the tower builders, William Beckford is perhaps the best known, famously plying his immense workforce with beer in a bid to get the men to work around the clock on a mighty and beguiling 300 footer which he called Fonthill Abbey.

Intoxicated as a result, they built one which promptly collapsed – and later a second which did much the same thing for much the same reason – thereby laying the foundations of a reputation for eccentricity which

Beckford has been unable to throw off after all these years. Mind you, when you set out to build what in its day would have been the country's biggest folly – not to mention by far the tallest house in Europe – you'd be foolish to expect to be viewed in any other way.

Just 10 years-old when his father died (so who can blame him?) Beckford inherited an estate in Wiltshire and a vast fortune, said to have been worth a million in 1770 with an annual income of £100,000. Enough to make him the richest little boy in the entire world, the family's wealth came from extensive sugar plantations in Jamaica and set the scene for a life of excess which few since have been able to match.

Though a commoner, he travelled in state and in style with a retinue comprising three footmen, 24 musicians, his doctor, his valet, a cook, two dogs – Mrs Fry and Viscount Fartleberry – and a Spanish dwarf (name unknown). Over a period of 15 years or so, his itinerary was impressive and it introduced him to a wealth of different architectural influences – for example, the monastery and abbey church of Batalha, Portugal – which were to make themselves felt when he settled down to design Fonthill.

More than anything else though, Beckford's Fonthill was to be enormous, centered on an octagonal tower 300 ft high but constructed by workers too befuddled with beer to worry about foundations (and working too fast to notice that anything was amiss). All in all, the place took six years

to complete – and just a few seconds to collapse. Like any authentic eccentric, Beckford shrugged off the disaster, contacted his bankers and called everyone back to have another go.

This time, he insisted, it was all going to be different, with better materials, a longer build-time to make sure everything was done correctly, and some proper foundations. And to be fair to Beckford, Fonthill Mk II lasted long enough for him to live in it, and for Turner to paint it so we know what it looked like. Eventually it did collapse, however, but only after it had been sold to the unfortunate John Farquhar, an untidy millionaire who clearly quite eccentric himself delighted in being mistaken for a tramp.

Before his arrival, however, Beckford had a marvellous time with the place, entertaining Lord Nelson on one occasion and on another, a trespasser who had somehow succeeded in scaling the seven mile long, 12-ft high walls which Beckford had built around the estate. But generally he held imaginary dinner parties beneath the octagon. The table would be laid for twelve, food and drink would be prepared for twelve guests, and twelve footmen would be detailed to stand behind twelve chairs – even though nobody but Beckford had actually been invited to sit down and eat.

When the time came to sell Beckford was virtually bankrupt, but happily sold the place on for a substantial £330,000 and moved to nearby Bath. He planned another tower there, this one to be a mere 154 ft tall and destined to stand in his garden at Lansdowne Crescent. Designed not by himself but by a proper, trained architect, H.E. Goodridge, it's still standing.

With two hundred steps to the summit, and crowned by an elegant replica of the Athenian Monument of Lysicrates, Goodridge's design incorporates a library and a chapel as well niches in the walls in which – it is said – the maids employed by the rampantly misogynistic Beckford were required to hide when he came past. In time the garden, exceedingly narrow but almost a mile deep, became a graveyard with a marble tomb erected for another Beckford dog (Tiny) and, once the legal niceties had been completed, to enable him to lie in unconsecrated ground a pink granite sarcophagus for her master.

Happily these days the tower is occasionally open to the public in the summer, at which time readers might like to visit the Black Castle at nearby Brislington. One of the west country's strangest pubs, and somewhat incongruous in its present suburban setting – though probably no less so than when it was built in the 1760s – it should appeal to modern environmentalists as it is constructed entirely from industrial waste.

It was built as a stable block for a local Quaker copper smelter called

William Reeve using spelter slag, a byproduct of the smelting process. A purplish-black stone which looks as if it has been boiled in brine, the material is light, tough and impermeable, an excellent building material, in other words, although its darkly sinister appearance has lent the pub the nickname of 'the Devil's Cathedral'.

SIR FRANCIS DASHWOOD (1708-1781)

John Bastard and the golden ball

The founding father of the notorious Hell Fire Club – although it's tempting to think that his fabled wickedness was contrived in order to compensate for his boring daytime job as Postmaster-General – Sir Francis and his friends originally gathered at the Eighteenth Century Medmenham Abbey in Buckinghamshire, hence the Club's other title 'the Mad Monks of Medmenham'.

Using the official title of the Order of St Francis, its members, a secretive group of apparently wildly dissipated aristocrats, were said to use the place to celebrate a black mass, delighting in performing acts of 'gross lewdness and daring impiety' on a desecrated altar whilst eating strange food served by naked girls on whom they later pressed their basest and most disgusting desires. The Abbey is also the place where, in 1777, after a massive £100,000 wager, the Chevalier d'Eon de Beaumont was declared by a jury to be female – and then discovered *post-mortem* to have been a man after all.

But in truth, most of the Hellfire stories that have come down the years are simply too corny or too daft to be true. That said, one is still pleased to find some evidence of Dashwood's other activities surviving down the road at West Wycombe.

As it happens there are still Dashwoods living there too, although these days it is leased from the National Trust, as it was here that Sir Francis chose to build his most lasting legacy, namely a series of fascinating follies around the house and park.

The strangest perhaps is the golden ball atop the Fourteenth Century church, a feature added in the early 1760s and still accessible by ladder. Large enough to seat six, it has unsurprisingly been adopted with glee by conspiracy theorists who insist that here too the Mad Monks performed their sinister rituals, whilst the trees in the surrounding park – they say – were planted in such a way as to form patterns of vulgarity when viewed from above . . .

Down below, Sir Francis also built a mausoleum (assisted by the wonderfully named John Bastard using funds provided by Lord Melcombe) to commemorate George III's emergence from madness. There are too, a variety of temples and another, wonderful flint-knapped church which on closer inspection turns out to be an elegantly decorated cottage built for one of the estate workers.

CLOUGH WILLIAMS-ELLIS (1883–1976)

Italy comes to Wales

Nearly eighty years after its inception and what its creator called 'a home for fallen buildings', the little village of Portmeirion, constructed on family land in Snowdonia using a combination of architectural salvage and a good dose of artistic licence this remains the best possible (and one would argue the most delightful) destination for anyone looking for a good reason to take a drive through Wales and the Marches.

The man behind it all, Sir Clough Williams-Ellis MC, was a gentleman but no amateur. Self taught but highly motivated and well skilled, when the former Welsh Guards officer was offered the chance to buy a wild and remote peninsular called Abar Iâ he at once saw in it the opportunity to use his professional know-how (and fees) to put his architectural theories into practice. Creating the fantasy village that we see today, he designed it and built it expressly to demonstrate that it is possible to develop a naturally beautiful site – and Abar Iâ is **very** beautiful – without resulting in its defilement or loss of amenity.

To do it his way took him 50 years and cost a fortune, but the ever pragmatic Sir Clough defrayed the cost by opening the main house as a small but luxurious hotel. W. Somerset Maugham came here in the 1930s, George Bernard Shaw and Bertrand Russell were habitués, and another regular, Noel Coward, penned *Blithe Spirit* during a fortnight's stay here in 1941. Most famously however, the place was to be immortalised more than twenty years later when the late Patrick McGoohan decided its location and atmosphere would be the perfect setting for his enigmatic (if occasionally incomprehensible) 1960s television series, *The Prisoner*.

Clearly inspired by the former fishing village and now long-fashionable Italian coastal resort of Portofino, Sir Clough furnished his peninsular not just with cottages and small shops but also columns and arches, a shell grotto, formal, terraced gardens and walkways, an elegant *campanile*, cobbled streets, fountains, pools and statues. The entire ensemble is painted in various pretty Mediterranean pastel shades and is set off by the sub-tropical plants, trees and shrubs which survive in the surprisingly frost-free micro-climate of this corner of the Welsh coast.

It sounds kitsch and it is, but it's also delightful, not least because of the wild beauty of the surrounding area and the incredible thoroughness of its overall execution. Portmeirion is no mere pastiche and Sir Clough's fallen buildings – including Jacobean stonework, Seventeenth Century plaster mouldings from an old Flintshire mansion, the famous Bristol Colonnade, fragments of R. Norman Shaw and even huge cast-iron radiators discarded during some upgrading work at Harrow School – lend the project an irresistible touch of class as well as an aura of timeless tranquility. Today most of the buildings are let as holiday accommodation but as one strolls around the village one finds a surprise at every turn – just as its creator intended.

THOMAS HOLLOWAY (1800–1883)

A touch of the Loire in the Home Counties

A self-made millionaire with a handsome fortune built on patent medicines, in 1871 Holloway invited readers of the journal *The Builder* to help him decide, 'how best to spend a quarter of a million or more' – a vast sum of money which in the event he was actually to double. The ideas flowed in (as you can imagine) but in the end it was his wife who came up with the right answer, suggesting that building a college for women at Egham in Surrey was the means by which Holloway's money would secure the greatest public good.

Nothing too eccentric about that, of course, just good old fashioned Victorian philanthropy – at least that's how it appeared until the architect came on board and the two of them got down to business.

Holloway selected William Henry Crossland (the pair were already co-operating on another philanthropic enterprise, a sanatorium at nearby Virginia Water) and whilst considering in what style they should build

Holloway fastened on a wildly flamboyant interpretation of French Renaissance architecture.

Inspired in particular by the Sixteenth Century Château of Chambord in the Loire Valley, the results are spectacular to say the least. At 550 ft long, well over a hundred yards wide and a third of a mile all the way round, Holloway's folly in the end proved to be quite considerably larger than the original and today, even when one knows what's coming, it still has the power to surprise anyone making their way through the overbuilt Surrey countryside.

Architecturally it can hardly hope to escape a charge of vulgarity, but it is appealing nonetheless, a slightly crazy confection of towers, cupolas and the most elaborate ornamentation which if nothing else, keeps visitors busy as they scan the stonework for yet more delightful details.

Formally opened by Queen Victoria, and built around two large quadrangles (if you can spare the time to walk around and find them you'll discover the carved heads which decorate the brick and white Portland stone exterior include not only Her Majesty's but a trio of Old Testament kings Joshua, Saul and Solomon, and the three prophets, Elijah, Moses, Ezekiel). Elsewhere are those of such diverse cultural luminaries as Handel, Dante, Shakespeare and Molière. Oh, and Mr and Mrs Holloway too of course, modestly tucked away in the lower quad.

As solid as it is extravagant, and now part of the University of London, Royal Holloway College is not only a fine memorial for its benefactor but also a perfect monument to the wealth, optimism and spirit of philanthropy which so characterised the Imperial age.

ECCENTRIC LONDON ARCHITECTURE

- In the south-east corner of Trafalgar Square, housed within an ornate lamp-post, the world's smallest police station has its own direct line to Scotland Yard and room inside for a single copper (The lamp itself, like its twin across the way, is a splendid multi-faceted glass orb popularly but wrongly believed to have graced Nelson's flagship HMS *Victory*).
- Five miles away from this, London's narrowest building, is the widest. The former home of the Royal Regiment of Artillery, Woolwich Barracks, with a façade over 1,000 ft in length is a

grand Classical parade of brickwork and colonnades which the architectural historian Sir Nikolas Pevsner favourably compared to the Winter Palace at St Petersburg.

- Woolwich is also now home to John Nash's extraordinary Rotunda, a highly original construction which started out as a tent in St James's Park, erected in 1814 as part of the celebrations following the defeat of Napoleon. Five years later, moving his masterpiece to Woolwich and replacing canvas and wood with copper and pale yellow brick, Nash converted it to a permanent structure.

- On nearby Shooters Hill, now surrounded by trees in a public park, a triangular folly some 60 ft high was erected in 1784 by Lady James. Constructed in memory of her husband, Sir William, whose 'superior Valour and able Conduct' won the day, its three hexagonal turrets combine both Georgian and Gothic elements.

- On the very edge of the City of London, on land originally purchased to bury the plague dead, an old folks' home called Sutton's Hospital has, since 1613, favoured 'decrepit or old Captaynes either at Sea or Land' and 'Souldiers maymed or ympotent'. In their retirement they are promised 'a full library and a full stomach and the peace and quiet in which to enjoy them both'.

- Close to the National Theatre, the OXO Tower is a more recent landmark, though few know the story behind it. In 1928 permission to build the tower was refused on the grounds that advertisements – in this case for a famous brand of stock cube then owned by the Leibig Extract of Meat Company – were not to be placed above a certain height. The architect, however, successfully argued that it was not an advertisement merely that his tower's giant windows just happened to be in the shape of Os and Xs.

- In Fleet Street there stands another rare survivor, this time of the Great Fire of 1666. Known as Prince Henry's Room, it is London's last complete timber-framed Jacobean townhouse and as such, a unique remnant of the medieval townscape. It doubles now as the entrance to Middle Temple (one of London's judicial enclaves, known collectively as the Inns of

Court) and marks the very limits of the cataclysmic event, standing as it does, only yards from the line where the flames were finally beaten back and extinguished.

- There is of course plenty more besides. In Phipps Bridge Road near Wimbledon, a flint-built sham castle masquerades as a family house; in Kingsbury, Ernest Troubridge built at least a dozen more. Soho Square has a miniature Tudor manor house at its centre and by Victoria Station, a tiny decorative shell-house was built by the French Government after the First World War in which to store garden implements used to maintain a triangular garden dedicated to the memory of Marshall Foch. The list goes on and, while to the visitor, London may appear familiar it hides its secrets well.

- But then how many Londoners know their city any better? Less than a mile from Hyde Park Corner stands the tallest folly in Britain. Built with the profits of the Great Exhibition of 1851 to celebrate the Empire, Queen's Tower is nearly 300 ft tall yet most passers-by never notice it and many locals don't even know it is there.

CHAPTER TWO

Inventors

SIR FRANCIS GALTON (1822–1911)

Darwin's dotty cousin

LONG-LIVED, academically distinguished (besides being a Fellow of the Royal Society, he founded a chair at London University) and exceptionally well-connected – Charles Darwin was a first cousin – it's Sir Francis Galton's misfortune to go down in history as some kind of a proto-Nazi with an overdeveloped interest in the overdeveloped bottoms of African ladies and a penchant for silly hats.

By contrast, in his day, he was accorded rather more respect, being recognised as a pioneering statistician, the founding father of the science of fingerprinting – something he somehow stumbled upon whilst quantifying colour-blindness in Quakers – and of IQ tests. Similarly his passionate promotion of the new science of eugenics – a word he coined himself – was accorded just as much respect in the rooms at the Royal Society as anything proposed within the same walls by his illustrious cousin.

But unfortunately for Sir Francis just as his enquiries tended at times to lead him down some very strange roads indeed – after his death he won the praise of Himmler – so his enthusiasm for collecting accurate data would occasionally leave him open to the charge of being more than a little barmy.

Who else, after all, would bother to invent a pocket-sized device in order to count the number of pretty women he met during the course of his working day? Or fit his house with an aircraft-style device to indicate and record when the loo was occupied? Or swear by the use of gunpowder as an emetic? Or indeed, to carry a brick around with him so as to have something handy to stand on when he needed to see over other people's heads?

That said, the 'pretty girl counter' more than paid its way once the keen statistician had got it home and started to manipulate the data. Using it to

draw up what he called a Beauty Map of Britain, which took many months of research out in the field, he concluded that London had the highest proportion of pretty girls. (Aberdeen had the lowest, although strangely the map was to prove a bestseller north of the border when it eventually went on sale.)

Unfortunately, the same counter was later used to measure the incidence of blue eyes and blonde hair, part of his scheme for advancing what he called 'racial perfection' – hence Himmler thinking him a 'great Englishman'. That is why no-one these days any longer dares dismiss Sir Francis as entirely harmless.

A keen and energetic traveller who would break raw eggs into his boots to soften the leather, Galton also attempted to put a figure on different national levels of dishonesty – concluding that the English were the most honest folk in Europe and Greeks the least – and even devised a way of measuring bottoms with a sextant after recognising that collecting data using a tape measure might be to invite hostility from the women in question.

Some of his other ideas require little explanation. For example, his advice about keeping your clothes dry in a storm was to take them off and sit on them. Others take a little more understanding, such as his complex mathematical equations for calculating the resemblance between two people, or the workings of the miniature pressure sensors which he had fitted to his dining room chairs in order (he said) to gauge how much his dinner guests liked each other.

Apparently, having noticed that guests who found each other engaging tended to lean towards each other when they talked (and that the reverse was true of those who disliked each other) Galton wanted to find a way of putting a value on the relationship. Whereas most of us would probably be content to observe how freely or not the conversation flowed between one friend and another and take an approximate measure from this, Galton used his pressure sensors to measured the inclination of each chair and, therefore, the level of engagement between one guest and the next.

Unsurprisingly perhaps for someone who claimed to have sprained his brain reading Mathematics at Cambridge, Sir Francis was also obsessive about his own cranial health and sought to maintain it with yet another invention, namely a perfect example of Heath-Robinson headgear in the shape of Galton's Universal Patent Ventilating Hat.

Based on his belief in something akin to medieval 'humors', this hat was fitted with a valve which was opened and closed using a rubber bulb that hung down conspicuously over the wearer's shoulder. Using this, the wearer could prevent his head overheating, thereby, as Sir Francis politely informed his hostesses at dinner, avoiding the possibility of embarrassing fellow guests 'by falling into a fit upon the floor'. Typically thoughtful, typically Galton.

SIR GEORGE RERESBY SITWELL (1860-1943)

Sir George lays an egg

Such an embarrassment that even his own children took steps to avoid dealing with him, the sheer volume of his ludicrous creations – a long list suggesting an entire lifetime devoted to exploring the unfeasible – means it is hard not to warm to Sir George Reresby Sitwell, Bart.

A man who, despite a clear interest in technological progress, banned electricity from his household until well into the 1940s (and restricted guests to just two candles each) he once expressed great disappointment at the non-appearance of a promised piece of jewellery when an acquaintance had quite clearly told him, 'I'll give you a ring on Thursday.'

Not that one would wish to spend too much time in his company, of

course, since it is a measure of the man that all house guests were on arrival shown a notice requesting them 'never to contradict me in any way as it interferes with the functioning of the gastric juices and prevents my sleeping at night'. It is also probably significant that his famous offspring Osbert, Edith and Sacheverell actually went so far as to invent a fictional yacht called the *Rover* so they could pretend to be away sailing on it to avoid unnecessary visits home.

Whether or not he missed them, Sir George certainly kept himself busy – attempting to barter for his sons' Eton College education with potatoes from his Renishaw Hall estate in Derbyshire, copying Chinese willow patterns from plates onto his herd of cows, and burying himself away in his seven separate studies where he would write singular monographs on strange subjects and experiment with a series of increasingly bizarre inventions.

On a visit to London he tried unsuccessfully to get the department store magnate Gordon Selfridges to stock one of the latter, his 'Sitwell Egg' which was a quite disgusting confection comprising a smoked meat 'yolk', compressed-rice 'white' and a 'shell' of artificial lime. This, the resourceful Baronet thought, would serve as the perfect portable snack for a gentleman on the move, but Selfridge clearly thought otherwise and Sir George sensibly turned his talents to a number of non-food items.

These included a musical toothbrush which played 'Annie Laurie' while the user brushed his teeth, a unique lead-suspended mosquito net which the 81 year-old insisted on using everywhere (even at home in the depths of a Derbyshire winter) and a miniature revolver which had been configured for shooting wasps.

Whilst not a single one of these ideas took off, the details of each was painstakingly documented in a book entitled *My Inventions*, one of literally dozens Sir George wrote whilst beavering away in his various studies. Others included such tempting titles as *The Use of the Bed*, *Lepers' Squints*, *The History of the Fork*, and *Errors of Modern Parents*. He sadly failed actually to complete a single one.

JEREMY BENTHAM (1748–1832)

Prison reformer fails to stop the rot

Better known as a philosopher than an inventor – and, like Sir George, too keen to move on to project No. Two before fully completing No. One – Jeremy Bentham nevertheless had a successful career as a writer and lawyer, and was the founder of University College London. In his spare time he also gave us the idea of the speaking tube, having pre-empted the

idea of the telephone by suggesting pipes be laid from one building to another in order that townsfolk could speak to each other without leaving home.

His other creations included the 'frigidarium' – a careful refinement of an Eighteenth Century ice house – for keeping food fresh, and what he called the Panopticon, a vast wheel-shaped jail of an avowedly progressive design. Emanating from Bentham's genuine interest in prison reform, this enabled warders to keep an eye on everyone from their station at the building's hub with the prisoners arranged in open-fronted cells along the spokes. Unfortunately, it garnered limited support from the British establishment, although London's Milbank Penitentiary was built along Benthamite lines. However, his design caught on in America and is still used today in many different states.

Bentham was also passionately interested in language, and coined a number of new words. Many of these we now take for granted, including 'codify', 'maximise' and 'international' although his attempt to have the British Isles officially renamed 'Brithibernia' happily came to nothing.

He kept his strangest theories until last however, namely the one based on his belief that dead bodies should be put to more practical use than being simply stuck in the ground. In particular, he felt that great men – amongst whom he clearly included himself – should be preserved and put on display to serve as an example to others.

He insisted every man could be reborn as his own statue if properly preserved. This would mean ancestral portraits could be replaced by actual ancestors, and mere paintings made to give way to actual heads. In middle-class homes, carefully preserved, successive generations could be artfully arranged on shelves or in what he called 'a moderate sized cupboard.' Alternatively, 'if a country gentleman has rows of trees leading to his dwelling, auto-icons of his family might alternate with the trees.' In such cases, Bentham stressed rather desperately, 'copal varnish would protect the faces from the effects of rain.'

Whether anyone ever tried this now seems doubtful, but clearly believing that by any definition he too was one of these great men – and one is inclined to agree that, on balance, he probably was – when Bentham died in 1832 he promptly had himself dissected for the benefit of science and his remains embalmed, stuffed, dressed and mounted in a smart glass case by the entrance to his new college in central London.

Unfortunately, with swagger stick in hand and top hat on head, things didn't go quite according to plan, and the head in question is not actually

Bentham's. That sadly proved to be no more durable than some of his barmier theories and (according to Bentham's physician Dr Southwood Smith) it lost its expression early on in the embalming process. Instead the good doctor, as the auto-icon's careful custodian for the first twenty years of its existence, commissioned a replica to be made in wax and it is this which sits staring at visitors today. The slowly-rotting original looks up grimly from the floor . . .

JOHN GAINSBOROUGH (1711-1788)

Sudbury's black sheep

But for his more famous brother, 'Scheming Jack' Gainsborough might have been forgotten, written off as just another Eighteenth Century conman – and perhaps deservedly. He was in many ways little more than a middling watchmaker from the pretty little Suffolk market town of Sudbury, one whose extra-curricular activities more often than not met with a singular lack of success.

Certainly he never lacked for inspiration for his new ideas, but application was never Gainsborough's strong suit and time and again he was left

sitting surrounded by the wreckage of an abandoned project observing, 'had I but gone on with it I am sure I should have succeeded . . . but a new scheme always came across me'.

Among these schemes were the design for a self-rocking cradle and another for a mechanical cuckoo, both said to have been built although no examples survive. Then there was his mechanical walking haystack although details of how this might have functioned (or why anyone should want one) are vague to say the least. Gainsborough also tried to fly using wings of beaten copper – a feat which earned him the soubriquet of The Sudbury Daedalus – but he was no more or less successful than a score of other Icarus wannabes who were active at this time.

Perhaps his best idea, however, was one of the earliest and something he cooked up for a neighbour while attending the town grammar school and which he called the 'apple-dumpling tree'. Ingenious, if somewhat labour intensive, this involved each apple on the tree being carefully wrapped in dough and 'by means of a chafing dish of hot coals and a saucepan' cooked *in situ* whilst still growing on the bough.

Given Scheming Jack's future, it is possible this was more a money-making venture than a serious invention, for whilst he was never short of ideas – and certainly he was mechanically highly skilled – he rarely had enough money for his projects and was constantly getting into trouble as a result.

His first watch-making business, for example, was up the road in Beccles but by 1743 notices were being placed in the *Ipswich Journal* warning readers that Gainsborough 'has greatly abused the interest of his friends, and carried off goods and effects given him in trust . . . [This notice is] to apprise all persons to whom he may offer any watch to sale or pawn, to stop the watch and give notice of same to Mr Tho. Utting, watch-maker, in Yarmouth . . . and they shall be paid for their trouble.'

Nor, given his family connections, should one be particularly surprised to discover that John also turned to the brush to get himself out of debt. Clearly here was a man who would try most things to turn a shilling, and today the White Hart at Nayland – an exceptionally pretty village on the River Stour between Colchester and Sudbury – enjoys the unique distinc- tion of having a pair of genuine Gainsboroughs on its walls, albeit by the wrong Gainsborough.

GEOFFREY NATHANIEL PYKE (1893-1948)

Sunk by a battleship of ice

Something of a real-life Professor Branestawm, Geoffrey Nathaniel Pyke made a fortune after being struck by how stupid-looking most stockbrokers were and concluding that making money in the City couldn't be that difficult. He must have had a point too, for the money came in so thick and fast that after a few short years he was able to quit the broking business for good and found his own school.

Expressly designed to be nothing like his old school (Wellington, which he hated) the fortunate pupils were encouraged to study whatever interested them, and lived free of punishment or reprimand. But unfortunately Malting House, Cambridge, soon ran into money worries, not least because Pyke himself had taken his eye off the ball and was already onto the next stage of his extraordinarily diverse career.

After a spell spent fitting sidecars to motorbikes to help the Spanish Civil War effort – these were kept busy running food to the front, and stretchers back from the lines – he joined Combined Operations in time for World War II where he devised a new kind of motorised sledge for the

Norwegian campaign. Sadly this arrived too late to help the Norwegians, but versions of it did much to advance polar exploration after the war.

His biggest project, however, was codenamed *Habbakuk*, an innovative design for a new class of immense aircraft carrier. With each vessel more than half a mile long and with hull walls 30 ft thick, the fleet was to be made of a kind of reinforced ice which its creator called Pykrete.

Pykrete was actually a mixture of water and wood pulp frozen solid, and Pyke insisted it was stronger than ice, a lot more stable and much less inclined to melt. Such a ship, he said, would be virtually unsinkable since bullets would bounce off it and even a fast torpedo would be likely to make only a slight dent in the side. Pipes circulating cold air through the fuselage would keep the hull permanently frozen, and any shell or torpedo damage could be put right using more wood pulp and water.

Hugely enthused by this idea Pyke had a vision of vast flotillas of such ships, clad in timber or cork and looking fairly conventional (if somewhat larger than the rest of the fleet). Pyke claimed the craft, suitable as transports, floating docks, and even aircraft landing strips, could simply sail into occupied ports, disable enemy vessels by spraying them with super cooled water – road and railway communications could be disrupted in a similar fashion – and then offload vast blocks of Pykrete to create blockades around the port once it had been secured.

Whilst many brass-hats distrusted the whole idea from the start (no, really they did) Pyke himself had a number of supporters in some very high places, including Lords Mountbatten and Zuckerman. The latter, as chief scientific adviser to the War Office, admitted Pyke was not a scientist, had a 'totally uninhibited tongue' and was often 'overwhelmed by the fantasies he created.' Nevertheless, he insisted, he recognised Pyke's value as 'a man of a vivid and uncontrollable imagination' and he clearly liked having him on board. As for Lord Louis, he went even further and seems almost to have made it his personal mission to ensure that Pyke was given a proper hearing by those in positions of high authority.

As an example of this, on one occasion he rushed into the Prime Minister's private bathroom with a lump of Pykrete and dropped it into Sir Winston's bath to demonstrate its resistance to melting. On another, he pulled out his revolver and shot a lump to demonstrate its toughness – although this particular demonstration backfired somewhat when the round ricocheted off and almost hit a watching admiral in the leg. Pyke himself had already demonstrated to a group of our American and

Canadian allies how well (compared to pure ice) Pykrete would withstand a blow from an ax.

To Mountbatten's credit the demonstrations went down well enough, and a prototype ship was actually built on a Canadian lake well away from prying eyes in the hope that it would last through that country's hot summer without melting away to dust. This it managed to do, but unfortunately the conventional war effort was moving swiftly on and the success of the Normandy landings in 1944 removed the need for Pyke's giant ice ships so *Habbakuk* was never fully put to the test.

Thereafter, the few years remaining to Pyke were not happy ones. The ideas kept coming, but interest in them – and it has to be said in him too – waned rapidly and, on 21 February, 1948, Pyke took to his bed-sitting room with a bottle of sleeping pills and a razor to remove his little goatee beard. It was a strange, sad end to an extraordinary life, but also one characteristic of Pyke if only because, even as he was slipping in and out of consciousness, he kept working away at some notes on his lap in an increasingly spidery hand.

PERCY SHAW (1890-1976)

Twinkle-twinkle, little life-saver

More a tinkerer than a big thinker, Percy Shaw nonetheless left the legacy of the 'cat's eye', the night-time road-safety device which has sold by the tens of millions since he patented the invention in 1934. It was his one big idea, but in his long life he was rarely idle and was always fiddling around with one little refinement or another with plans for advanced, rubber backed carpets and a new kind of petrol pump.

From humble Yorkshire stock (Shaw was one of fourteen children, and he never forgot it) he worked as a welder, mill-hand, machinist and boiler maker before going into the road-mending business and devising an early mechanical road roller using an old Ford engine and steering column, a pair of radiators and a set of truck tyres. He made some money with that one, and an estimated £11 million from his life-saving cat's-eye, much of this at pre-war values. And while it isn't quite true to say Shaw remained unchanged by his fortune he certainly didn't go quite so overboard in the usual way of so many instant millionaires.

For example, Shaw decided that the modest terrace house in which he had grown up when his father was a labourer in Halifax was more than sufficient for a man of means and remained his home for 84 of his 86 years. Curiously, he also refused to fit any curtains because he enjoyed the view of the street, or splash out on carpets because he felt they merely provided somewhere for tobacco ash to hide.

He also kept his old stable workshop because it was a place he fondly remembered having spent much of his childhood there helping his father. Indeed, in a sense it always remained the hub of his operation, being the place where he made his first cat's-eye and countless other little innovations.

But eventually Shaw's operation completely outgrew his father's old workshop with his company at one point manufacturing and selling an incredible 30,000 cat's-eyes every week. Even then insisted the brand new Reflective Roadstuds factory be built next door to his workshop, and such was his reverence for his childhood home that when further expansion threatened a sycamore tree in the garden he ordered the new manufacturing space to be built around the tree which can still be seen growing out through the factory roof.

Old Percy wasn't entirely without extravagance, however, and in common with many a self-made Yorkshireman he ordered a more than usually luxuriously-appointed Rolls-Royce for himself, equipping it with electric seats (a complete novelty at the time) and a filler cap which could be opened automatically. Stocking his cellar with crate after crate of his favourite Worthington's White Shield beer, Shaw was also reportedly something of a telly addict, and had three sets tuned to three different channels at a time when one was still considered a luxury.

Later it was said he had six of them in his small house, one set piled on top of another, but somehow this just doesn't sound like Percy.

BRITAIN'S ODDEST JOBS

- The Constable of the Tower of London has, for more than six hundred years, had the right to claim a barrel of rum from any naval vessel using the river. (He is also entitled to any livestock which falls off London Bridge, to a penny for each leg of any animal which falls into the moat, and to charge pilgrims tuppence as they arrive to visit the shrine of St James.)

- Still in the Tower, the Raven Master is responsible for ensuring that the ravens don't leave the Tower as tradition dictates the Crown will fall if they do. It's a relatively easy task these days, however, as the birds all have their wings clipped to prevent them flying away.
- The Lord High Admiral of the Wash (a vicar's son from Hunstanton in Norfolk) technically owns all the land from the high-tide mark to wherever he can throw a spear. Charged with maintaining the security of the Wash, he owes his position to his descent from Henry L'Estrange Styleman Le Strange, the Le Strange family having monopolised the post since feudal times.
- Female herb-strewers were traditionally employed to scatter sweet-smelling petals wherever the monarch processed, within the royal palaces, as well as outside on the streets, and today the Fellowes family still claim the hereditary right to do so on behalf of their eldest unmarried daughter.
- The Queen's Remembrancer, invariably a senior member of the judiciary, is responsible for collecting so-called 'quit rents' such as the pair of knives – one sharp, one blunt – payable each year for a small scrap of land in Shropshire, and the six horseshoes which comprise the rent for tenement (now long gone) in London's West End.
- The Lord of the Manor of Scrivelsby is the official Queen's Champion and since the Conqueror's day has been charged with presenting himself at Westminster before each coronation. He's there in order literally to throw down the gauntlet on the monarch's behalf and to do battle with anyone present who wishes to contest his or her accession to the throne. The Dymoke family of Lincolnshire has held this gauntlet – and the associated honour – since 1350.
- The office of the Lord Great Chamberlain – one uniquely shared between three families, who take turns as a new monarch ascends the throne – has been in existence since Norman times. In return for various minor ceremonial duties

the holder is entitled to demand anything the sovereign wears at a coronation (including the undergarments) also his or her bed – and the throne. The present holder is the Marquess of Cholmondeley with Lord Carrington's family and the Earl of Ancaster's currently awaiting their next turn.

CHAPTER THREE

Men (and The Odd Woman) on The Move

ROBERT NICHOLL MATTHEWSON (1866–1928)

Steam car swansong

STRANGE to think now, but there was a time when steam-power was all the rage – back in 1906 the so-called Woggle-Bug, a racing version of the popular Stanley Steamer, smashed the World Land Speed Record at 127.66mph – and for a while steam even looked set to rocket past any of its new-fangled petroleum or diesel-powered rivals.

Certainly out in the Empire 'Scotty' Matthewson of Swan Park in Alipore, Calcutta, seemed to think so. Calcutta was at this time the capital of British India, and this wealthy and successful engineer had his own theories about what use boiling water vapour could be put to, setting out to demonstrate them using one of the most singular examples of new-car design ever seen.

For reasons best known to himself, Matthewson decided to have his new car built by Lowestoft-based Brooke Marine, a well-known Suffolk boat company, and insisted the overall design theme be that of a giant wooden swan. In fact, the company already had some experience of automobile manufacture (its 1901 three-cylinder model featured a small bowl in the centre of the steering wheel in which to store the owner's goggles) but they subcontracted the body out to a Kings Lynn company, Savage, which at the time was England's best-known manufacturer of steam-powered fairground rides.

This perhaps explains the slightly comical aspect of the car Matthewson ended up with, a far from sedate four-wheeled device featuring a gigantic

swan's head and body which were carved and coloured to simulate the effect of feathers. The swan's eyes formed the car's lights, and the beak could be made to spit steam and hot water in order to clear pedestrians out of its path. As a finishing touch the bird's nostrils could also be made to steam like a dragon's whilst emitting a highly convincing swan-like hiss. Matthewson finally asked for eight Gabriel organ pipes to be fitted inside in order that tunes could be played using a keyboard fitted to the rear compartment, these to be powered by the exhaust gases produced as the car trundled along.

Completed at vast cost and shipped to Calcutta, the car was an instant hit with its new owner (and his family, so that a children's version soon followed). But alas, it was soon banned from the streets by the local authorities who tired of clearing the crowds which invariably accompanied its every journey. Doubtless they also found slightly offensive the car's most outrageous trick, a feature which 'Scotty' delighted in demonstrating in the fashionable surroundings of Maidan Park.

It was here that Calcutta's Edwardian elite would gather to promenade in their carriages and cars, and as such it was the perfect place for the Swan Car (using a concealed dump valve at its rear end) to drop splats of whitewash onto the road, thereby making the whole ensemble as much like a real swan as possible. Nice one.

HON. MRS VICTOR BRUCE (1895–1990)

Girl's Own Paper comes to life

The first woman to ride a motorbike, the first to have an accident, the first to win the Monte Carlo Rally Coupe Des Dames, and the first Englishwoman to fly solo around the world, Mildred Mary Easter Petre demonstrated a fearless fascination with speed and danger when she was very young. From the age of just fourteen or fifteen, she was spotted racing along on her brother's motorbike with her beloved collie in the sidecar.

Repeatedly hauled into court for speeding – she was also the first woman in this country to be fined for speeding – she once told the dumbfounded bench that going slowly made her tired. But as she grew older Mildred graduated from two wheels to four and from country lanes to race tracks. A rare example of a woman succeeding in a man's world, she eventually captured no fewer than seventeen different world speed records.

A regular competitor in continental road races, eschewing overalls in favour of a smart skirt, blouse and pearls ('I'm no women's-libber and don't at all approve of that sort of thing') Mildred and her husband later set a 10-day endurance record at Montlhéry near Paris and famously drove further north into the Arctic Circle than anyone had ever done before. Then, in 1929, she drove a four-and-a-half-litre Bentley for 24 hours, capturing yet another world record for single-handed driving (averaging 89 mph) and one which has still to be beaten by another lady driver.

However, the best of all came a year later when, spotting an airplane for sale in a shop window, she conceived a plan to fly solo around the world even though at this point she had never piloted an airplane before. At the suggestion of the Minister of Aviation she reluctantly agreed to book a few lessons first, but only after buying the aircraft in question, a diminutive two-seat biplane called the Blackburn Bluebird. It cost her £500 and securing her licence after just two weeks of lessons she was ready to depart, setting off from Heston Field (now a service station on the M4) to become the first person, male or female, ever to fly from England to Japan and the first to cross the Yellow Sea by air

After learning Morse Code, Mildred felt she was taking things a bit far for an amateur, and decided to leave her parachute behind in order to save weight. She took care to pack a spare propeller, however, also a dicta-phone to record her thoughts whilst travelling and a small shoulder bag

containing a compass borrowed from her husband, her passport and logbook, a bottle of water, a sun hat and an evening frock in case anything special came up in the way of social occasions.

In less than four days, she was over the Persian Gulf, having already had several close brushes with disaster. Outside Belgrade, for example, she had been following a train (by way of navigating) and then nearly crashed into the side of a hill as it disappeared into a tunnel. After this, clearing oil from her windscreen somewhere over Turkey, the hapless aviatrix accidentally kicked one of the rudder pedals going into a spin from which she was able to recover less than 500 ft from the ground.

Later still, finding herself over colonial Hong Kong on Armistice Day, Mildred naturally cut her engines in order correctly to observe the customary two-minutes' silence. But perhaps her riskiest manoeuvre was landing on a dried-out salt lake in Persia where, unfortunately, the salt crust broke pitching her aircraft forward onto its nose. With the prop broken to smithereens – thank goodness for that spare! – the pilot had to be rescued by a band of local tribesmen.

In Indo-China, the Chief of the Air Force awarded Mildred the prestigious Medal of the Order of the Thousand Elephants of the White Parasol in recognition of her being the first person to fly solo from London to Hanoi, but in Japan she was forced to deviate from her planned route by a law forbidding anyone to look down on the Emperor. She fell foul of regulations in New York too, after flying at not much more than street level the length of Broadway and then circling the Empire State Building. After this, the cops were waiting for her when she finally put down at Glenn Curtiss Airfield, but fortunately she managed to talk her way out of it.

Eventually, after a total of five months and for the final leg of her voyage into Croydon, Mildred was accompanied by fellow female aviator Amy Johnson and once home it was clear that she'd caught the flying bug good and proper. Once safely down, and having briefed the press, she joined a flying circus for a while before founding her own company, called Air Despatch, successfully proving that in-flight refuelling was a practical reality by managing to remain aloft for an extraordinary three days on the trot.

GEORGE OSBALDESTON (1787–1866)

'Squire of All England'

Apparently unable to sit still for long and in such a hurry to be a Master of Fox Hounds that he bought the Earl of Jersey's pack whilst still an under-graduate, Osbaldeston was so keen to get moving that he left Oxford without taking his degree. He also left the Commons, where aged 25 he was Member for East Retford, without making even a maiden speech.

Eventually Master of the great Pytchley, but equally at home on the gallops at Newmarket or shooting in Norfolk, here was a man who – barely five feet tall and with a pronounced limp from a bad fall – clearly lived for sport and who strongly maintained that a week was wasted if he hadn't spent a good six days of it in the saddle.

Proud to have killed a hundred partridges with a hundred shots, to have put 40 bullets into a single ace of diamonds from 30 yards, to have played billiards for two days and two nights without a break, and cards from dusk to dawn at a hazardous £100 a trick and £1,000 a rubber, he therefore set aside most of his time for riding and before long had notched up some impressive records, not a few of which probably survive to this day.

Osbaldeston was, for example, so energetic in his riding that having exhausted his hounds he bought a pack of mastiffs in the belief that they might be better able to match his stamina. He was wrong. Similarly in 1831, after he had wagered someone that he could ride 200 miles (or 50

times around the long course at Newmarket) in 10 hours or less, he unhesi-
tatingly picked up even better odds from a man who challenged him to do
it in less than nine.

By this time, Osbaldeston was approaching 45 and many thought he was
past it, but he clearly relished the challenge and set to organising the
attempt immediately. Arriving in the early hours a few days later, resplen-
dent in his purple and white racing silks, he eventually succeeded in
completing the course in just eight hours and 42 minutes. To do it he had
changed horses 26 times, 'pitting' just once himself to consume a cold
partridge washed down with brandy and water and, when it was over, he
galloped off to the Rutland Arms in the High Street for a stiff drink and a
hot bath.

By all accounts not a nice man, he was nevertheless popular with the
public as a result of such derring-do and his likeness still hangs in the
National Portrait Gallery. Osbaldeston could even be quite chivalrous on
occasion, providing (it appears) it involved getting back on his horse.

Most famously, having seen a young lady rebuffed at a ball when she
attempted to compliment another on her beautiful orchid, he galloped off
into the night, covering 25 miles of rough country in four hours to visit a
distant conservatory whose owner was then persuaded to assist him in his
quest. Reappearing as the ball was drawing to its close, mud-spattered,
exhausted, sweaty but somehow glorious, Osbaldeston presented the
surprised young lady with an even finer specimen and led her onto the
floor.

Sadly, there was no money riding on it this time, however, because by
now he could certainly have done with some. As old age beckoned, his
family fortune was all but gone, yet one suspects George would have had it
no other way. Life after all, was for living, even if in the end he was reduced
to existing on an allowance in St John's Wood, London, with the horses,
the wagers and the orchids all just a dream.

ALAN JAMES MONTAGU-STUART-WORTLEY-MACKENZIE, EARL OF WHARNCLIFFE (1935-87)

Comedy into farce into tragedy

Dead at 52, and at various times a drummer in a rock band, an able
seaman, racing car driver, pub landlord and garage mechanic, Lord

Wharncliffe has a story suggesting the sort of reversal of fortune which the public still finds irresistible. (Much like John Hampden Hobart-Hampden-Mercer-Henderson, the 8th Earl of Buckinghamshire who died in 1963 in the knowledge that his ancient titles would pass to someone called Fred who formerly worked as a gardener for Southend-on-Sea council earning just £9 a week.)

Certainly, the quadruple-barrelled Montagu-Stuart-Wortley-Mackenzie had a lively time of it, although as his obituary in the *Daily Telegraph* was quick to note, his colourful career was eventually 'overcast by a series of tragedies'. The worst of these was when his daughter Lady Joanna was killed in a car-crash at the age of 21, soon after Wharncliffe emerged from prison having served six months for causing another road accident in which a pub landlady was killed.

The offspring of conventional upper class and actually quite formidable parents – his mother had established her own munitions factory during the war – the 4th Earl's early career was pretty standard: Eton and then a spell in the Royal Naval Voluntary Reserve. After this he enrolled at the Royal Agricultural College at Cirencester and succeeded his father as Master of the Ecclesfield Beagles. It's true that at the College he joined the famous Beards' Society, the members of which took a vow never to shave again, but there were few other signs of eccentricity. (In any case he quit shortly afterwards because his chin itched, prompting the Society's secretary to admit that he was 'rather annoyed to think that a peer of the realm should act in this way'.)

After this Wharncliffe joined a band as a drummer, and upon returning to the family estate outside Sheffield, elected to run a pub rather than play the traditional role of local squire. He reportedly shot dead a cat he found in the kitchen. During this time, he also ran a car-repair workshop in the backyard, and as a keen driver, notched up an impressive series of bans for various different motoring offences.

These culminated in a three-year disqualification for drink-driving, after which he took another vow – not to drink any more – although this quickly went the way of the beard one. As a result, within just 15 days of the ban being lifted, he was rushed from the roadside to hospital, remained in a coma for six weeks and at one point was actually declared to be clinically dead.

Recovering slowly, and eventually being considered fit enough to stand trial, he tripped over his crutches and broke his leg again before finally being found guilty of dangerous driving. Receiving the expected custodial sentence he reportedly coped well with his incarceration, and even persuaded a fellow jailbird to play the role of valet.

JESTYN REGINALD AUSTEN PLANTAGENET PHILIPPS, VISCOUNT ST DAVIDS (1917-91)

Hail the Pirate King!

Whilst it was clearly cars for Lord Wharncliffe, it was life on the water which did it for the 2nd Viscount St Davids, and he spent a lifetime campaigning for the restoration of Britain's inland waterways whilst diving for shells in his spare time and living aboard his yacht *Tortoise* moored on the Regent's Canal in central London.

Another Old Etonian – and a lieutenant in the Royal Naval Voluntary Reserve after serving in the Army during the war – Lord St Davids is these days remembered as a committed socialist (so too, he insisted, was Bertie Wooster) and founder of the Regent's Boat Club. Housed in an old Grand Union barge *Rosedale*, and seeking to introduce London's youth to the delights of messing about on the river, the club was run on strictly democratic lines and offenders against its code were typically offered a choice of expulsion, confinement in the brig, or 'a good smack on the seat'.

Club members, several hundred boys and girls over the years, also became somewhat notorious on the main stretch of the canal for mounting rattling-tin raids on any passing canal boats. Dressed in full pirate regalia and with their Pirate King in attendance, their objective was to raise money to fund the building of a proper clubhouse to replace the ageing barge. This they finally managed to do in 1977, moving into a compact but pretty convincing little waterside castle which had been designed for them by Colonel Richard Seifert, who at the time was London's most prolific architect.

The powerful influence of Lord St Davids also ensured a memorable first day for the new clubhouse. It was officially opened by the Lord Mayor of London who in traditional pirate fashion was then held in the 'dungeon' – actually the club's boat deck – until a suitable ransom was paid.

When he wasn't sailing or raiding, the thrice-married St Davids was a keen parliamentarian, campaigning against fireworks and against the extension of the hereditary principle – despite the fact that he was an hereditary peer himself, as was his own mother. (She sat in the Lords in her own right as Lady Strange of Knokin, so the two of them enjoyed the distinction of being the first mother and son ever to sit together in the Lords – or rather not quite together as they found themselves on opposing sides of the house.)

ANTHONY, LORD MOYNIHAN (1936–91)

Keep on running

Constantly on the move in quite a different sense – a treasured possession was a tacky brass plaque declaring, *of the 36 ways of avoiding disaster, running away is the best* – the 3rd Baron Moynihan, in the words of his *Telegraph* obituary, provided 'ample ammunition for critics of the hereditary principle'.

Despite a tendency to describe himself as an authority on rock and roll on the questionable grounds that he could play both the banjo and bongo drums, a more accurate rendering of his CV would include occupations as diverse as brothel-keeper, supergrass and drug-smuggler, whilst for relaxation Anthony Patrick Andrew Cairne Berkeley Moynihan apparently liked nothing more than causing trouble and then fleeing the scene.

He started young: first escaping his father's wrath upon being discovered consorting with a strip-club waitress, and later that of his father-in-law after taking a swing at wife number one, a part-time nude model. Then, after a brief spell lying 'doggo' in Australia, he returned to Soho to wed a belly-dancer, something which he later insisted required him to convert to Islam.

The two of them briefly ran a nightclub in Ibiza, and then a themed bar near Bromley – the theme being that of a Spanish bull-fighting arena – after which he underwent a second religious conversion, this time to the Baha'i faith, whilst on a belly-dancing tour of the Middle East. A spell as a chauffeur for slum landlord Peter Rachman brought him back to London, and then in 1965 his long-suffering father passed on, thus elevating Moynihan to the junior ranks of the peerage and giving him a seat in the Upper House.

As was perhaps only to be expected, this chapter of his career was no more successful than the preceding ones, and on one occasion a long-suffering colleague in the chamber was forced to interrupt one of Moynihan's lengthy, ill-structured speeches with a request that he not continue on the grounds that 'the noble Lord has bored us stiff for nearly three-quarters of an hour'.

Clearly it was time for Moynihan to be on the move again, and pretty soon he was – when it emerged that he had a total of 57 outstanding charges against him including purchasing a Rolls-Royce with a rubber cheque, fraudulent trading and a certain amount of being up to no good at a gaming casino. Returning first to the Iberian peninsular, he then hopped across to the Philippines when threatened with extradition.

Here he landed on his feet as his latest wife – yet another belly-dancer – had family connections with a chain of massage parlours which he was soon brought on board to help run. At the same time, both back home and in Australia, Moynihan's name came up in connection with a number of more serious crimes including drug-running, prostitution and eventually even murder. Fortunately for Moynihan he successfully sought and obtained the protection of his 'best drinking chum', President Marcos.

Unfortunately, Marcos had his own problems and following a coup Moynihan was coerced into saving his own skin by acting as an informant for both Scotland Yard and the US Drug Enforcement Administration. Temporarily safe as a result, he made an attempt to sell his great-grand-father's Victoria Cross as he needed the dough before returning to Manila and resuming his life as a pimp. Cheerfully telling the press 'I just sit back and collect the money, the girls do all the work' he always insisted that he would eventually return to the UK to clear his good name and to resume his seat in the Lords where he planned to take the Labour whip.

Happily this never happened, and it will surprise no-one to hear that upon his death there was considerable confusion as to whom, exactly, would inherit the title.

HUGH CECIL LOWTHER, EARL OF LONSDALE (1857–1944)

The Yellow Earl

The great Lord Kitchener had his Rolls-Royce painted yellow so that he would be recognised and given immediate priority by policemen directing traffic around the streets of London. When the Duke of Sutherland assumed the presidency of the Royal Automobile Club in Pall Mall it was his practice to have one of four Rolls-Royces fired up at all times and ready to go so that he could make a speedy getaway whenever he chose to do so. And at the rival Automobile Association, Lord Lonsdale, his Grace's opposite number, seemed to combine the two by having not just the cars painted yellow but literally everything he could get his hands on.

Today of course, the AA still sports the same colour on its vans and breakdown trucks, insisting the heightened visibility is a big plus when assisting a member stuck on the hard shoulder in bad weather. To the Earl, however, the bright hue was clearly also a matter of stamping his own identity on the organisation, for back home at Barleythorpe in Leicestershire he had previously commissioned a new yellow livery for his servants, ordered his carriages to be painted to match, and even bought new yellow wheelbarrows and yellow cardigans for the groundsmen on the estate.

Despite the AA connection, however, Lonsdale was actually rather more interested in horses than these new-fangled horseless carriages and, in Barleythorpe, he had one of the best studs in the country. His hunting skills were not inconsiderable – he was Master of the Cottesmore. But in the field particularly, he was never one to suffer fools, especially any members of the local peasantry who came between him and his quarry and was known to be a bit quick with the whip when it came to dealing with either man or beast.

On one occasion, he ordered a groom to shoot dead a favourite new hunter which had refused to jump a hedge. When the poor man declined to do so (aware that said horse was a good'n' and had just cost his employer £500), Lonsdale went to the yard and stood over the groom until he had done as he was told.

Knowing all that, one wonders why anyone would have anything to do with him but, in 1908, the Earl had a mammoth £21,000 bet with the millionaire banker, J. Pierpoint Morgan, that a man could walk around the world whilst supporting himself by selling postcards and finding a wife along the way. It fell to one Harry Bensley to prove him right or wrong.

The terms of the wager were complex to say the least but, in the end, it all came to nothing. After six years and with just seven countries left to go, war broke out after the assassination at Sarajevo of Archduke Franz-Ferdinand, and Bensley came home to join his local volunteers. After the incident with the horse, no-one would have been surprised had a disappointed Lonsdale reached immediately for his whip (or even his gun) but somehow Bensley lived to tell the tale, perhaps because, with Morgan now dead and the world at war, all bets were off so his Lordship hadn't lost a penny.

Known to all as the 'Yellow Earl' (but never to his face: he preferred 'Lordy') Lonsdale's name lives on as a brand of clothing and because of his close association with the famous porcelain and 22ct gold Lonsdale Belts for boxers. (The 'blinging' originals were provided by him when he was president of the National Sporting Club.) He also gave his name to a cigar, a pretty substantial *corona* which, though somewhat smaller than the range-topping Rothschild, is suitably plutocratic for a man of his undoubted ego.

JEAN HAMMOND

Barns full of bubbles

If you want to squeeze more than forty cars into a single barn you have to have a very big barn or some very small cars. Luckily down in rural Kent Jean Hammond has both, as well as a cowshed round the corner containing even more miniature three- and four-wheeled curiosities.

Jean, together with her late husband Edwin, started collecting micro-cars' in the mid-1970s and these days admits it's hard to know exactly how many she's actually got. 'About 45,' she reckons, 'depending on how you count them. That's complete cars but I never really know whether to include the basket cases when I get asked that one.'

The names of some of them, such as Messerschmitt, Heinkel and Vespa, are immediately recognisable albeit probably not in connection with motor cars. Other badges bearing the logos of AC, Allard and BMW are equally familiar, though they are more often seen on machines at the other end of the performance scale. Most are much rarer items, however, many literally unheard of by all but the most well-informed motoring enthusiasts.

Tiny cars like the Opperman Stirling, the Cassalina Sulky, the Frisky, Goggomobil, Bamby, Tourette and Peel were built in appropriately tiny numbers and whilst some (like the Opperman and Goggomobil) look rather like real cars scaled down, others make little attempt at conventional styling and almost glory in their toy-like bubblecar designs.

The collection started with a 198cc Eire-built Heinkel which the Hammonds bought in the mid-1970s for their six-foot, teenage son Andrew, in an attempt to lure him away from motor bikes. At the time, Jean herself was running a mammoth 7.2 litre Jensen Interceptor, but found the Jensen crowd 'a bit stuffy' unlike micro-car enthusiasts whom she considered far more friendly.

The motor madness continued. 'After that we bought another Heinkel, a German one this time, then an old Scootacar which our daughter found being used as chicken coop, and the collection began to grow.' The French Flipper, for example, was won in a raffle and one of the two baby Fiats was bought at a Boy Scouts' jumble sale. A pair of very sorry-looking Empolini vanettes were donated to the collection by a pizza-delivery company in London. Perhaps the saddest of all though is the local Kent-built Cursor which was fished out of the Medway after being dropped in the drink by vandals.

More than the quality of the engineering, it is the innovative approach of the microcar designers which most attracted Jean and her husband.

In Germany, where from 1945 new uses had to be found for many ex-aircraft and munitions factories, designers particularly needed to box clever to work and survive on such a small scale. Thus, Messerschmitt produced a car which looked like a fighter aircraft's cockpit because that's what they knew best. Similarly, although the little Isetta looks eccentric these days, it was arguably the car which saved BMW in the immediate post-war period.

In the forties and fifties, creative problem-solving at low cost became paramount in micro-car design, so that cars like the Hammonds' Maico Champions (they have at least three, including a Morris Traveller-style 'woodie' version) were designed to be built using only five body pressings. Incredibly, and despite matching front and rear panels and doors which are interchangeable, the 300cc Champion manages to look like a miniature 1950s Porsche.

Another car in their collection, the Kleinschnittger, was similarly designed to be dropped behind enemy lines by parachute, whilst the splendid Velorex with its imitation-leather body has an air of glamour to it having been smuggled out of Cold War Czechoslovakia by a student fleeing to the East. More recently, it's been joined by another refugee, a toothpaste-pink Trabant from the former East Germany, which was presented as a gift to a popular teacher by his grateful pupils each of whom autographed the bodywork as a memento for his retirement.

Today, few bubblecars are commonly seen and Jean Hammond's rarest must be the aforementioned Opperman Stirling, the sole survivor of only two built. Its twin was shown at the 1958 London Motor Show where it attracted considerable interest from the public but never made it through to production. Instead, perceived as a rival for the forthcoming Mini, it was killed off by the big components manufacturers who were too scared to touch it in case they upset the then-mighty British Motor Corporation.

TRANSPORTS OF DELIGHT

- More than three-quarters of a century ago *Autocar* magazine earnestly set out to road test a new type of passenger vehicle called the Holverter whose curious steering mechanism enabled all four wheels to turn in the same direction in order that said vehicle could inch sideways like a crab.
- In 1864, retired cavalryman Colonel Pierpoint designed the world's very first traffic island and had it installed in St James's Street, London so that he could reach his club without incident. Built at his own expense, the invention worked a treat until one day, as he paused to look over his shoulder at his pride and joy, the Colonel was struck by an approaching cab.
- In 1911, Isaac Smyth managed successfully to patent a design for a motor car fueled by gravity, although there is no evidence that he ever managed to get it to work.
- Covering 38,000 miles in three and a half years, Stan Mott is the only person ever to have circumnavigated the globe by go-kart. (It's also been done by a Rytecraft Scootacar, one of the smallest vehicles ever to complete the journey being based on a fairground dodgem.)
- Chrysler launched its 1934 Airflow saloon after deciding that most cars were aerodynamically more efficient when travelling backwards.
- Driving his 11CV Citroën for nineteen hours every day for an entire year, Frenchman François Lecot covered a quarter of a million miles between 23 July, 1935 and 22 July, 1936.
- In 1906, Charles Glidden drove his modified Napier 4,900 miles along the railway lines from Boston, Massachusetts, before becoming derailed just fifty miles from Mexico City. Similarly, in 1930, two Americans drove backwards all the way from New York to Los Angeles.

- In 1933, the architect and engineering visionary, Buckminster Fuller, built a safety car called the Dymaxion. Of an entirely novel design, and with only one-wheel-drive, it unfortunately crashed killing everyone on board
- In 1948, thinking it worthless, Henry Ford II turned down the chance to buy Volkswagen. (Mind you it must run in the family: his grandfather Henry Ford I, turned down the opportunity to build the Spitfire because he was convinced Hitler would win the war).
- Effete pianist, Liberace, spent £300,000 gold-plating his 1931 Cadillac roadster and fitting mink carpets. It later failed to sell for £55,000 at an auction in Buxton, Derbyshire.
- The Delauney Belleville limousine, built for Tsar Nicholas II in 1910, had no less than eight foot pedals. (Lenin preferred Rolls-Royces and, despite his egalitarian posturing, kept at least nine of them for his personal use.)
- TNT, dynamite, nitro-glycerine and petrol were just four of the ingredients in a 1931 land speed record attempt. It failed.
- Using parts from his Honda Accord, musician Bill Milbrodt has made 15 instruments including the Doorimba and Exhaustophone.

PERCY SHOLTO DOUGLAS, MARQUIS OF QUEENSBURY (1868-1920)

Carbarians at the gate

In 1887, the Comte de Dion claimed to have won the world's first-ever motor race, despite the fact that his steam-powered 'quadricycle' was the only vehicle entered. A few years later, Sir Edward Nichol removed Edward VII's coronation robing room from the Palace of Westminster in order to have it rebuilt at home as a garage. Thereafter, and for many years, the price alone ensured that the motor car remained the exclusive plaything of the rich, but it was by no means true that everyone among the upper classes welcomed the new-fangled devices onto the streets, and not just because their noise and choking smell threatened to overwhelm the horses.

For its part, *The Times* thundered against those it referred to as 'motorious carbarians', while farmers complained about the dust kicked up by their wheels. In the US, a more militant lobby proposed in all seriousness that new automobiles be fitted with explosive devices set to detonate automatically should their owners allow the cruising speed to rise above walking pace. And closer to home, Percy Sholto Douglas, 10th Marquis of Queensberry, went straight to the heart of the matter by seeking the legal wherewithall to shoot dead all motorists he saw on the grounds that simply by existing they endangered the lives of his family.

To this end, he told bystanders en route to Hammersmith that he fully intended equipping himself with a loaded revolver 'for the purpose of shooting dangerous drivers'. Although there is no evidence the mad marquis actually saw his plan through, it was nevertheless an idea enthusiastically endorsed by at least one Justice of the Peace.

OSBORNE DE VERE BEAUCLERK, DUKE OF ST ALBANS (1875-1964)

A bird on the arm is worth two in a bush

Osborne de Vere Beauclerk, 12th Duke of St Albans, Earl of Burford, Baron Vere of Hanworth and of Heddington – 'Obby' to his pals – is one of no less than five modern-day dukes whose ancestors were fathered by Charles II with his mistresses, the most famous of them being Nell Gwyn.

Obby's eleven predecessors, it is generally agreed, were neither illustrious nor particularly accomplished, and more than a few of them were clearly mad. Most recently, the 11th spent at least thirty years of his life in a Home Counties asylum, while his brother mounted a serious attempt to burn Eton College to the ground. When the 12th came along, it must therefore have elicited a sigh of relief, the 11th's half-brother being a tad odd in his habits but never actually, clinically insane.

That said, and like many latterday dukes, Obby made it clear pretty early on that he wished to play as small a part as possible in public life, deciding, for example, to boycott the Queen's coronation in 1953 when as Hereditary Grand Falconer of England he was refused

permission to attend with a live falcon on his arm. (Palace officials tactfully suggesting he wear a stuffed bird instead, but he certainly wasn't having any of *that*.)

He left it late to get married as well, becoming engaged to Beatrix Beresford, Dowager Marchioness of Waterford, at the age of 43. She had half a dozen children already but Obby elected not to attempt an heir in the belief that his family's tradition of madness was actually hereditary. (If asked, he pointed out the 9th duke's wife was the most likely cause of it all). Bizarrely, he had no such qualms about illegitimate offspring, however, and left so many of these that he was reportedly never entirely sure who many of them were.

For much of his life Obby stayed at home in Ireland, gaining a reputation for interrupting the sermon each Sunday by periodically shouting 'rubbish!' from underneath the handkerchief with which for some reason he liked to conceal his face whilst catching forty winks. Occasionally, he would visit London in order to drop into the Turf Club or Brooks's in St James's Street, where Newman, the hall porter, was expected to wind his watch for him on the way in. But suddenly in 1958, at the age of 83, Obby decided to change the habit of a lifetime and hit the road for real.

When he did this his choice of destination – the Americas – was perhaps less surprising than his chosen modes of travel: a rough-and-ready cabin aboard a freighter crossing the Atlantic, followed by a Greyhound bus ridden coast to coast. The Americans clearly loved the idea of a 'gen-u-wine' English lord slumming it in this way, and he reportedly received no fewer than sixty eight proposals of marriage before setting off to explore South America. This he did by second-class train, presumably by this time recognising the reality that such was the state of the Beauclerk fortune that when the time came for his heir to inherit he would get a string of titles but little if anything else.

BENJAMIN O'NEALE STRATFORD, EARL OF ALDBOROUGH (1808–1875)

Proto-balloonatic

When it comes to matching nobility to mobility plenty of aristocrats have sought to make their own contribution to the history of flight, but there's arguably none so poignant as the largely wasted efforts, and indeed life, of the Right Honourable Benjamin O'Neale Stratford II, 6th and last Earl of Aldborough of the Palatine of Ormond

It's true that he didn't lose his life flying – unlike Lord Llangattock's son, the Hon Charles Rolls (of Rolls-Royce) who was the first Englishman to die in an aeronautical accident when the tailplane snapped clean off his Wright Flyer. Or, for that matter, like the celebrated 'Flying Duchess' of Bedford did between the wars. She found the altitude cured a buzzing in her ears (she was stone deaf) but sadly disappeared on a routine flight in 1937, after which it was discovered that she'd had the word *WOBURN* painted in huge letters on the roof of her ancestral home to help her navigate. This proved quite an embarrassment when several departments of the Secret Services moved into the Abbey during the war.

Like them, Aldborough lived to fly and, like his fellow lord, Brabazon of Tara, he felt strongly that 'to go up in a balloon is the only way to go into the air like a gentleman.' His problem was his timing, although his determination was never in any doubt.

In fact, for nigh on twenty years after resigning a captaincy in the 1st The King's Dragoon Guards, he shut himself away at Stratford Lodge near Dublin with the intention of building the largest balloon the world had ever seen.

Attended by just one manservant, and with his meals prepared and

cooked in the capital and sent over with the mails, His Lordship beavered away night and day, with his one aim being to fly his 50-ft diameter monster across to England and then France. With a subsidiary title of Viscount Amiens, he had already bought a patch of land on the banks of the Seine on which to put down.

In 1853, Aldborough changed his plans somewhat. Hearing that the Crimean War had started, he agreed to extend his journey eastwards in the belief that he could use his balloon as an aerial platform from which to take potshots at the Russian army. He wisely resisted the temptation to follow the lead of the Austrians who, four years previously, had attempted the first aerial bombing in history. (On that occasion, a flotilla of around 200 pilotless, timebomb-carrying hot-air balloons was launched against troops defending Venice but the Austrians had to take cover after the wind changed direction, sending the balloons back over their own troops with disastrous results.)

Unfortunately, Aldborough's new-found patriotism soon lost its purpose when peace broke out, long before he'd had time to complete his balloon. Then, as if that wasn't bad enough, Stratford Lodge caught fire, possibly as a consequence of arson, with the good lord locked in his bedroom and apparently unable to find the key. Eventually, the door was battered down and he escaped without injury, but the fire had by this time taken hold and threatened to destroy not just the Lodge but also the adjacent 'balloon house'.

Indeed, by the time it was brought under control, Aldborough's dreams lay in ruins, the elaborate silk envelope of his vast balloon damaged beyond repair and his already shaky grip on reality weakening by the hour.

For some time, he carried on an even more reclusive existence in the remains of the burned out hangar, quietly weeping over the corpse of his project. Aldborough then retired to an hotel room at Alicante, Spain, which he refused to leave and was sustained by no more than room service. Rarely seen in public again before his death, he surfaced occasionally only to check out of a room when it was filled with dirty crockery and glasses and to move into another. Lord Aldborough died aged 67 having never actually taken to the air.

MARY COVE (1885–1906)

Ballooning over the Brontës

In the main, visitors to Haworth are there only because of the Brontë girls and their brother, and one suspects that few ever wonder about the early death of Mary Elizabeth Cove – if indeed they even notice her headstone with its detailed little carving of a basket slung beneath a balloon.

Unlike the Earl of Aldborough, Mary (known as Lily) at least managed to get aloft. Her trouble was coming down – which sadly she did for the last time on 11 June, 1906.

Mary had been flying high after becoming addicted to the new sport of ballooning at an early age, and learning about it under the expert tutelage of her boss, a celebrated aeronaut called Captain Bidmead ('the hero of four hundred balloon ascents'). Once hooked, she decided – unexpectedly for one of her sex – to try her hand at parachuting.

Here Bidmead could help again, since he was, not entirely coincidentally, 'the hero of eighty-three parachute descents.' What Lily might not have known was that at least two of those went badly wrong: the first when his parachute failed to deploy and he dropped 80 ft (until a steeply sloping roof broke his fall rather than his body) and the second when his 'chute became entangled with the rigging of the balloon and he was dragged for several miles and through a number of hedges before being unceremoniously dumped into a canal.

However, the two of them set off together to explore the effects of airflow and of gravity with Lily learning the basics whilst strapped to the Captain as he flung himself out of the basket. After several assisted jumps he considered her ready for the big one, and having checked her parachute himself, Bidmead arranged for her first solo drop to coincide with the annual Haworth Gala.

You can see how this was going to turn out, can't you? Dressed in a white blouse and smart, black breeches, Lily hurled herself out of the balloon at 700 ft. Then, after releasing herself from the parachute, she dropped like a stone to her death before a crowd of hundreds of horrified onlookers. Precisely why the tragedy occurred has never been discovered, although the Captain's theory was that as a non-swimmer drifting towards a reservoir, poor Lily had misjudged the distance and attempted to jump onto dry land. Either way, it was a sad end for a courageous young person, and a highly eccentric one for any Edwardian let alone a female.

WOULD YOU BUY A CAR FROM THESE MEN?

- Henry Ford was clever, no question, for by the end of the Great War, half of all the cars in the world were Model-Ts. But to get a true measure of the man, you need to read his own private newspaper, *The Dearborn Independent*. Run with the express purpose of campaigning against Jews, it showed him to be a committed anti-Semite who blamed them for all manner of ills, including short skirts and jazz music. Today, the founder of the automotive giant enjoys the dubious distinction of being the only American citizen to be mentioned by name in Hitler's *Mein Kampf*.
- Enzo Ferrari was honoured by fascists too, Mussolini bestowing on him the title *Commendatore* although there's no evidence that, like Ferdinand Porsche, creator of the Volkswagen Beetle, he provided comfort or material support to a dictator. Ferrari certainly ruled like one, however. He was an autocratic, self-confessed monomaniac who hired and fired world championship-winning drivers like they were nobodies. For years, he also insisted his wife and mother share a house even though they clearly couldn't stand the sight of each other. They lived at opposite ends of the building, and his mother eventually choked to death on a hardboiled egg although fowl play was never suspected....
- By contrast, over the border, Ettore Bugatti was clearly popular with his workers, and knew each of them by his first name. Here again though there is no suggestion that *Le Patron* was anything but a fantastically tricky piece of work. Most of all, he knew he was right – about everything. He modestly christened his first child L'Ebé after his own initials, refused to build any cars with left-hand drive (despite the fact that he was in France) and opposed the introduction of numerous technological advances including front-wheel brakes and independent front suspension. Best of all, in 1936

when his workers went on strike, he flounced off in a huff to Paris and never came back to the factory.

- Finally, there's our own Walter Owen Bentley who, for a long while, insisted that these new-fangled motorcars were 'disgraceful vehicles that splashed people with mud' but then changed his mind the minute he tried one for himself. Like Bugatti, the great W.O. is generally described as a good employer, although it was said that if he found a youngster in the plant doing something he didn't like he would, like the fabled Basilisk, fix them with a stare so penetrating that they would never grow any taller. (Apparently if he also removed his pipe from his mouth, the miscreant might actually shrink.)

CHAPTER FOUR

Troglodytes, Hermits and Moles

JAMES WHITAKER WRIGHT (1846–1904)

Gun in hand, poison in pocket

THOUGH all traces of the house itself have now more or less gone, little-known Lea Park near Godalming, Surrey was the creation of a larger-than-life financier called James Whitaker Wright.

A self-made, self-publicising millionaire, he employed literally hundreds of navvies to landscape his park in a style befitting an authentic Eighteenth Century grandee. Any hills Wright felt were inappropriate were removed and new and better ones created. He also ordered the planting of many acres of lowland forest and excavated a dramatic quartet of lakes, one of which conceals Surrey's one and only underwater ballroom.

Wright hailed from Cheshire (although he affected an American accent) and was bent of course, eventually being sentenced to seven years for no fewer than 24 counts of fraud at the Old Bailey. Even then, he managed to cheat the public one more time by taking a cyanide capsule immediately he was sent down. (Incredibly he had a loaded gun in his pocket too, but clearly chose a quieter, more discreet way to go.)

Before this dismal end, Wright was really on a high, however, and today what remains of his elaborate scheme is still one of the most beguiling and beautiful man-made landscapes anywhere in the Home Counties even if, alas, what has been renamed Witley Park is no longer accessible to the public.

Anyone lucky enough to gain entry to the 500 acre walled estate, however, will find Wright's immense stable courtyard still intact. Other

survivors include a few decorative eye-catchers and temples scattered around the park, a boathouse designed by Lutyens, and an incredible eight acres of walled kitchen garden. Also beautifully landscaped and with its trees now mature, the garden and its carefully crafted contours have been softened by the years. With giant flowering shrubs everywhere it has at last matured to match Whitaker Wright's dreams.

As a finishing touch to his million-pound-plus scheme (and this is at late Nineteenth Century prices), Wright imported a gigantic bronze sculpture of a dolphin's head from Italy. Indeed, so gigantic was it, that when it was brought up to the estate from Southampton docks, the contractors had actually to lower the entire road in order to get it to fit under one of the bridges which lay along the route.

Whilst this perhaps gives some small indication as to the scale of Wright's ambitions – and the scope of his landscaping operation – it is nevertheless still not enough to prepare the visitor for what lies beneath one of his vast ornamental lakes.

Reached via a secret door in a false tree, through a dark, dank tunnel, down a spiralling ramp and a subterranean flight of steps, along another tunnel – this one flooded, requiring you to take a boat trip some 40 ft or more below ground level – across a lake to an artificial island and yet another staircase which takes you down below the water level, Whitaker's underwater ballroom is, in truth, too small to hold a dance.

It is, however, remarkable; somewhere for guests to have a quiet cigar while watching fish, and occasionally even swimmers who disport themselves overhead. There is a further tunnel leading to another artificial island where, on summer afternoons, Wright's lady guests could take tea.

WILLIAM JOHN CAVENDISH, DUKE OF PORTLAND (1800–1879)

Any colour you like so long as it's pink

Working on a far larger scale than even Whitaker Wright, William John Cavendish Cavendish-Scott-Bentinck, 5th Duke of Portland, was at one time said to have employed 15,000 workers to build follies on his Welbeck Abbey estate in the area of Nottinghamshire which we still call the Dukeries.

Cavendish's creations included an underground ballroom and three different libraries, all of them painted pink. He also gave each of his workers an umbrella and a donkey on condition that they (and all tenants living on the estate) never spoke to him or doffed their caps in his presence. Anyone who encountered the Duke in the park at Welbeck was instructed to pass by him 'as they would a tree'. Similarly all instructions were issued to staff in writing, with principal rooms at Welbeck fitted with two separate letter boxes for incoming and outgoing mail.

As shy and reclusive as all this suggests, His Grace is said to have seriously considered building a tunnel so that he could travel unobserved to Worksop Station more than three miles away. He is also known to have refused the Order of the Garter twice because accepting it would have required him to put in an appearance at Court. For a short while however, before coming into his inheritance, Cavendish-Scott-Bentinck was something of a man about town, an officer in one of the smarter regiments, and the Member of Parliament for King's Lynn. As it happened, the 3rd Duke had been Prime Minister in 1783 and then again from 1807 to 1809, Home Secretary before that and some time Lord President of the Council.

Cavendish's accession to the dukedom quickly changed him, however. Although he must have been familiar with the rhythm and life at Westminster, it took him a full three years to take up his seat in the Lords. We know now that this, in part at least, might have been because he was

kept busy at Welbeck, stripping all the rooms of their furniture, carpets, pictures and wallhangings – fortunately, these were stored rather than sold – before moving into a suite of just four or five rooms in the west wing.

He also instructed his staff, presumably by letter, to order hundreds of gallons of pink paint, sufficient wig boxes to fill an entire room (all of these to be coloured green, and each containing a wig) and, according to his socialite cousin, Lady Ottoline Morrell, insisted on commodes being fitted in all of the rooms he had recently vacated.

Mostly though, Cavendish was interesting in digging and with an army of several hundred Irish navvies imported for the task, he was soon hard at work creating a vast complex of subterranean spaces. These included the aforementioned ballroom – which was big enough to be useful, measuring 160 ft by 64 ft and able comfortably to accommodate 2,000 revellers. There was also a 250 ft long library, a vast, glass-roofed observatory and one of the largest billiard rooms ever seen with room for perhaps half a dozen tables.

All well and good, one might think, but then also singularly strange for a man who literally *never* entertained at home, and who kept 100 horses stabled (with 45 grooms on standby) even though he was never known to ride. Similarly, Cavendish also ordered the construction of a vast new indoor riding school, nearly 400 ft long and 110 ft wide – it was lit by

8,000 individual gas jets – which almost certainly remained unused until his death.

In all, no fewer than eight tunnels were excavated beneath the estate, totalling between three and fifteen miles depending on whom you listen to and with most of them linking these various underground developments. Because, sadly, there is scant physical evidence that the previously described route through to Worksop Station was ever actually completed, the longest is thought to be a 1¼ mile stretch running between the Coach House and South Lodge.

On Cavendish's rare trips to London, the strangeness continued, with staff at Harcourt House in Cavendish Square ushered out of sight so he could step unobserved from his carriage. At the back, he had an extra-ordinary 200-ft long screen erected around the garden, constructed of wrought iron and frosted glass. This was a full 80 ft in height to prevent anyone catching a glimpse of him promenading around the lawn.

Here and at home in Nottinghamshire, His Grace would habitually sport a minimum of two overcoats, a 2-ft high top hat, and trousers held a few inches above his ankle by knotted string. Ducal top coats were ordered three at a time, and in different sizes so that one would fit snuggly inside another. He would also carry an umbrella at all times to hide behind should anyone attempt to start a conversation. Finally, Cavendish also required his kitchens to keep several chickens roasting round the clock so that, at any hour of the day – and regardless of where he was at the time – one would always be ready in case he felt the need of a hot snack.

Whilst he was said to hold a candle for the singer Adelaide Kemble, it will surprise no-one to learn that the Duke died unmarried. Described after his death as 'vast, splendid and utterly comfortless' Welbeck Abbey, with his eccentric additions still intact, was eventually let to the Army which painted over the pink and, until 2005, used it as a staff college.

BRITAIN'S MOST ECCENTRIC COUNTY

- Historic Rutland was eradicated at the insistence of Whitehall beancounters in the 1970s but reinstated more than 20 years later at the behest of its few but vociferous inhabitants.

- At its heart, a small county town for a small county, Oakham is also the birthplace of a small man: Jeffery Hudson who, just 18 in high in 1628, hopped out of a pie presented to Charles I (*and wasn't that a dainty dish to set before the King?*). Its most famous landmark is the castle's Great Hall which contains hundreds of horseshoes bearing the names of every monarch and nobleman who has passed this way, a tradition harking back to William the Conqueror whose farrier lived here nearly 1,000 years ago.
- The county's greatest pile, Burley-on-the-Hill, home to the astonishingly profligate Duke of Buckingham and the Earls of Nottingham, was where the king was treated to the afore-mentioned dwarf pie – just the sort of high jinks which explains the eagerness with which the humourless Puritans battered the place down during the Civil War. Eventually rebuilt with the magnificent 200-ft long colonnade we see today (mimicking St Peter's in the Vatican) the 250-room palace was later acquired by the Man from Del Monte, entrepreneur Asil Nadir who paid £9 million for it before fleeing back to Cyprus. More recently, it's been converted into flats.
- The village of Cottesmore dates back to 1666 and gives its name to Britain's oldest and grandest hunt. It is said that the behaviour of Cottesmore's aristocratic members gave rise to the expression 'painting the town red' when a few young blades did precisely that to the town of Melton Mowbray after a good day out in the field and a few too many stirrup cups before setting off.
- On to Exton where the splendidly-named Henry Noel-Noel, ancestor to the Earls of Gainsborough, ordered the construction of 'a plastered pleasure house of a most refined and elegant Eighteenth Century manner'. It was called Fort Henry and was built on a stretch of ornamental water where it can still be seen today. Once it was finished, His Lordship liked nothing better than to re-enact famous sea battles, observing and ordering the proceedings from the battlements as miniature men-o'-war crewed by his servants did battle on the water below.
- Like an immense wedding cake, Harlaxton Manor is probably

Britain's maddest stately home (now part of the University of Evansville and full of Americans) and the nearest thing we have to the fantastical fairytale castles of Mad King Ludwig of Bavaria. It was built in the Nineteenth Century by Mr Gregory Gregory who, lacking family and apparently having no friends, devoted his entire life to the conception and construction of his dream house and, once it was completed, died there a happy man.

HON. CHARLES HAMILTON (1704–86)

Yet another hermit wanted, apply within

The ninth and youngest son of the 14 children born to the 6th Earl of Abercorn was another who so liked the idea of hermits that he offered to pay anyone £700 to live in a cave on his Painshill Park estate at Cobham, Surrey. In exchange they were expected to spend seven years wearing only camel hair and growing a beard, but unfortunately the only applicant for the job found himself bored to distraction after barely a fortnight and went off in search of some conversation and a good pint of beer.

As is so often the case with these things, Hamilton's enthusiasm was fired by his Grand Tour and first manifested itself in 1738 when he leased some two hundred acres of semi-barren heathland close to where the M25 now passes beneath the equally unpleasant A3. From this unpromising start – but ably supported by a share in his father's vast fortune – the Hon. Charles was determined to create a landscape which was both picturesque and fun to be in, taking as his starting point the paintings of artists such as Claude Lorrain, Salvator Rosa, Poussin and Panini.

As a starting point, the flat Surrey countryside was something he rightly viewed as in need of a complete remodeling and his first objective was to clear the site which had been one of Henry VIII's many deer parks. To increase its fertility he burned the existing vegetation down to the ground, digging in the resulting piles of ash and having his men grow turnips on the land which in turn were fed to sheep. Their droppings over time raised the level of nutrients in the soil, which was a slow process but like everything Hamilton undertook it seems to have achieved the desired result in the end.

A keen gardener and avid plant collector, Hamilton then imported

phenomenal quantities of rare and exotic species whilst planting a great variety of different trees and shrubs, including magnolias, pines and the inevitable rhododendrons. At the same time, and at immense expense, the park was landscaped with new valleys to open up the right kind of vistas and hills constructed to block off the wrong sort. A 19-acre serpentine lake was excavated, around which were arranged an imaginative series of architectural features.

Never one to do things by halves, Hamilton's follies included a grotto, a highly fashionable ten-sided Gothic temple, a Romanesque mausoleum, a ruined abbey, a Turkish tent, another temple (this one dedicated to Bacchus) a Chinese bridge, a hermitage for the aforementioned boozer, and a wonderful red-brick prospect tower which can still be seen today by anyone travelling south on their way to Guildford who chooses to look left at the right moment.

With such a long list you could be forgiven for wondering whether the workforce ever got around to designing a house for the site. The answer is yes, but only just. In fact, even the early drawings for this weren't completed until 1774 and, by the time the architect Richard Jupp really got his shoulder to the wheel, Hamilton was long gone, having been forced to sell the estate so that the house, when completed, was for the estate's next owner, Benjamin Hopkins.

As for Hamilton, having exhausted his portion of his father's fortune and now crippled with arthritis, he moved to Bath a few years ahead of that other great builder of dreams, William Beckford. Creating what Horace Walpole called 'a fine place out of a most cursed hill' had taken him 35 years and left him virtually broke. Worse still, perhaps, eventually even the park itself was to fall into ruin – a tragedy, for it was one of England's greatest gardens. Fortunately in the 1980s, almost the entire site was rescued by an independent trust and today its restoration is well underway so that Hamilton has his monument at last.

JAMES HAMILTON, MARQUESS OF ABERCORN (1756–1818)

Everyone loves a lord . . .

. . . Although in the case of John James Hamilton, 1st Marquess of Abercorn, it seems no one loved the lord quite as much as did the lord himself.

Very much one to stand on ceremony – and quite unwilling to forgive anyone who neglected to do so – this was the man who, even back in the days when he was plain Mr Hamilton, insisted on being addressed as D'Hamilton, Comte Hereditaire d'Abercorn, well ahead of inheriting any such title. When he did inherit an earldom, he successfully petitioned a busy Prime Minister to elevate his wife-to-be to the rank of an earl's daughter (which she wasn't) apparently in order that he wouldn't be seen to be marrying beneath himself. His second wife of three, she left him in the end, at which point he insisted she elope in his carriage, complete with his coat of arms on the doors, on the grounds that 'it ought never to be said that Lady Abercorn left her husband's roof in a hack chaise'.

Transport arrangements clearly played quite a role in Abercorn's daily life, and Sir Walter Scott was one of several acquaintances who gleefully told the story of how one day he had encountered a retinue of no fewer than five carriages, numberless outriders in full livery and at its head a man on horseback bearing the blue ribbon of a Knight of the Garter. This, it seemed, was simply the Hamiltons out for a little afternoon's constitutional.

Back home, things were equally formal with the housemaids required to wear white kid gloves before touching his lordship's bed linen and the other servants expected to rinse their hands in rosewater before Abercorn would accept anything they had touched. But perhaps the strangest thing about Abercorn was that, whilst he was a keen and generous host, and entirely happy for his guests to enjoy every luxury whilst staying in his Middlesex home at Bentley Priory, he would at other times exhibit a reclusiveness verging on misanthropy.

Thus, whilst reportedly enormously keen to pay host to literally anyone with a senior title or a claim to fame, the Marquess went so far as to send money to an up-and-coming authoress, Jane Porter-Hyde (to cover her expenses in getting to the Priory) but then, having observed her arrival from behind a curtain, slipped out through another door and refused to return until she had been and gone.

JOHN BIGG (1629–96)

Riches to rags . . . and leather

At Dinton near Aylesbury are two memorials to John Bigg, one an engraved portrait and the other a strange shoe. A scholar, Bigg was a native and inhabitant of the parish, and in his younger days acted as clerk to the lawyer and regicide Simon Mayne. More commonly called the 'Dinton Hermit' and not without means, he is thought to have been haunted by the Civil War and its aftermath – in particular his employer's decision to sit as a judge at the trial of King Charles I and his premature death in the Tower when a vengeful Charles II found his mark among the signatures applied to the royal death warrant.

In truth today many of his eccentricities would likely have earned Bigg a diagnosis of depression or breakdown, but in those simpler times he merely retired from public life and moved into a cave close to his former employer's home Dinton Hall.

A hundred years later, of course, he might have found employment (had he wanted it) as a professional hermit for one of the noblemen who fancied the idea of a tame, if hirsute, recluse to decorate their landscaped parks. But clearly Bigg preferred the real McCoy, and although he refused to beg for alms he no longer worked and was instead sustained by the charity of local people who fed and watered him for nearly 30 years.

Bigg's peculiarities included a very singular mode of dress, the aforementioned shoe, for example – the twin of which is in the Oxford Ashmolean – ably demonstrating the way in which he chose to mend his

clothes. With no change of apparel in his cave, wear and tear on the few clothes he possessed was naturally considerable and, before long, his appearance began markedly to decline. Bigg's response to this was to fasten a fresh piece of cloth or leather over any holes which appeared, thereby quickly building up the thickness of fabric until it was maybe ten or twelve layers deep. The result was not simply a patchwork effect, but rather a mass of scraps thrown together so that each item of clothing came to comprise literally hundreds of individual pieces.

Bigg was still a young man in his early thirties at the time of his withdrawal from society, and indeed his engraved portrait shows quite a handsome fellow – albeit one eccentrically dressed with a twin-peaked hood to his cape and a number of leather bottles slung from his waist. Apparently the bottles were to contain the milk and intoxicants – strong ale and small beer – which he received from local donors, his only other requirements being bread and spare fragments of cloth and leather which he eagerly sought from visitors and quickly sewed into place about his person.

HON. HENRY CAVENDISH (1731–1810)

London's very own Trappist

Like a perfect prototype for the barking mad scientist, Henry Cavendish remains all but unknown outside scientific circles despite having discovered the composition of water and of atmospheric air. He was also described by no less an authority than Sir Humphrey Davy (who designed the miners' lamp) as a great man 'acute, sagacious, and profound, and, I think, the most accomplished British philosopher of his time.' However, because he was somewhat backward in coming forward, Cavendish frequently left others to claim the fame for discoveries that were rightly his.

The grandson of the 2nd Duke of Devonshire, and as such phenomenally rich in later life, he spoke to almost no-one and never lost the habit of thrift, perhaps as a result of being kept short of money by his father until he was well into middle-age.

When living with his father close to Hampstead Heath, Cavendish was, for example, known to attend Royal Society dinners with no more than five shillings about his person (this being the exact cost of such a meal to the Society's Fellows). He even did this after inheriting around a million pounds – a huge sum at a time when a year's rent on a house in Grosvenor Square, Mayfair would have been barely £300.

Born abroad but educated at Peterhouse, Cambridge, Cavendish studied mathematics for four years before turning to chemistry and then physics. Thereafter he corresponded frequently with the Royal Society (continuing to do so for nearly 50 years) and also with his own servants having taken steps to guarantee his privacy by equipping his houses at 11 Bedford Square and in Clapham with a complicated system of internal mailboxes, double doors and even additional staircases to deter any of them from attempting to contact him in a more direct fashion.

Cavendish's mind, clearly, was always on higher things than human intercourse. He was not at all interested in his money, and on one occasion threatened to close all his accounts when a bank employee called on him to ask what to do with the £80,000 of interest which had accrued to him over several years.

Indeed, in only one regard was the Hon. Henry at all extravagant, and that was in his decision to maintain two different houses in London, one of which was gradually transformed into a vast library of scientific volumes and journals. Generously, he allowed other scientists free and easy access to this, although strangely he never borrowed from it himself without first checking that it was OK to do so (deferring to his own full-time librarian) and being sure to sign a chit to say which volumes he had taken.

In his own mind, however, all of this was anything but extravagant as the second house clearly served a quite separate purpose. It is true both were generously furnished with pictures, linen and everything else required to ensure they were equally comfortable places in which to live, but whilst the Bedford Square house was dedicated to knowledge already attained – hence the yards and yards of shelving filled to bursting – the house in Clapham celebrated the spirit of scientific enquiry yet to be undertaken.

Piled high with scientific instruments, its purpose was to further the owner's own private investigations and to this end it was equipped with a 'transit room' for astronomical observations, a platform in the garden for monitoring the weather, and a fully-equipped laboratory downstairs which one visitor recalls being 'stuck about with thermometers, rain gauges et cetera'. Cavendish also employed a mathematical instrument maker at the house on a salary of £65 per annum, this in addition to the usual complement of seven indoor and outdoor staff.

Described by a colleague as 'shy and bashful to a degree bordering on disease', Cavendish was nevertheless not entirely reclusive all of the time.

He occasionally entertained – guests were offered a leg of mutton every time, with nothing on the side – and as previously observed, he regularly attended Royal Society dinners although at these he was extraordinarily ill-at-ease.

Always at great pains to ensure he was not approached by anyone he didn't know, Cavendish tended to hover just outside huddles of conversation, talking to himself in strange, high pitched tones. Most obviously he could not bear to receive praise for his work and, on at least one occasion at the home of Society President Sir Joseph Banks, literally ran from the room and straight home to Bedford Square when a stranger made the mistake not just of addressing him but also of daring to look him directly in the eye.

Unsurprisingly, Cavendish died alone and unmarried. Prolonging life, he told his doctor, would only be to 'prolong the misery'. After his death, it was discovered that he had more bank stock than anyone in the whole of England. Nearly £1.2 million of this he left to his cousin Lord George Cavendish and the fact that his heir spent just a tiny proportion of it (£70,000) acquiring a townhouse in Piccadilly – Burlington House, now the Royal Academy – provides some idea of the value of such an inheritance at this time. More of it was later spent building London's first ever shopping mall, Burlington Arcade, but apparently only in a bid to prevent passers-by from throwing oyster shells and other unpleasant detritus over the wall and into Lord George's garden.

As for the Hon. Henry, whilst clearly a strange and lonely cove, he hopefully would find some small comfort in the fact that Burlington House is now home to a number of other learned societies in addition to the RA, including the Geological Society of London, the Linnaean Society of London, and – closer to his heart – the Royal Astronomical Society and the Royal Society of Chemistry.

JAMES LUCAS (1813–1874)

In a kitchen near Hitchin

Bright, well-read and, until the death of his mother, something of a dandy, James Lucas rapidly earned his reputation as Hertfordshire's leading hermit after boarding up the windows of his family home near Hitchin and refusing to come out ever again.

For three months, his only company was his late mother, whom he had carefully embalmed and laid to rest in a Snow White-style crystal coffin in the drawing room. He reluctantly surrendered this grisly exhibit only when the local constabulary forced the issue and insisted on removing the corpse for a more conventional burial. Unfortunately, with Lucas already overcome with grief, their incursion was enough to tip him over the edge and into galloping paranoia. Dressed conventionally, but later in little more than a blanket held closed by a meat-skewer, armed with every offensive weapon he could find, and with yet more homemade fortifications added to the house to prevent anything similar happening again, Lucas retreated to the kitchen where he apparently remained for the next 25 years.

Choosing not to wash, cut his nails or trim and comb his hair, Lucas soon burnt the furniture so he could sleep on a bed of ashes. (The fire-

places were never swept either, so that at his death, the room was apparently thigh-deep in ash.) From then on he kept cheese, herring and gin in a basket slung from the ceiling, to keep it safe from the many rats which soon joined him in his strange gaol, and his only companion was a horse. When this died, he went into mourning again, reportedly ordering a new blanket and a hat for himself (both white) to mark the occasion.

So far so bonkers, and yet the obvious diagnosis of Lucas' insanity was withheld in 1851 following his examination by the Commissioners of the Board of Lunacy. 'Far from being insane,' the Commissioners' report reads, 'the Hermit is a man of the most acute intelligence.' Others found him dirty, however, 'not partially or temporarily dirty (wrote one) but dirty comprehensively and permanently. His hair is dirty, his scalp is dirty, his face is dirty, his hands and arms are dirty, his body, legs, feet . . . ' You get the idea.

Unusually for a hermit, he was not entirely averse to company, although he showed a marked preference for tramps and other hobos over the many society types who came to gawp at him through the boarded-up windows. Thus Charles Dickens was chased away with a shotgun, Lucas' reward for such threatening behaviour being a cameo role in Dickens' *Tom Tiddler's Ground* as Mr Mopes 'an obscure nuisance [and a] slothful, unsavoury, nasty reversal of the laws of Human Nature'. A grand lady of a certain age was similarly dismissed by Lucas as 'an old ewe dressed lamb-fashion if ever I saw one.'

By contrast, anyone needy was treated with the utmost courtesy and given gin and small change before they left, cash for this arriving at the house courtesy of a £25 a month standing order with his bank. (It was always small change though, since Lucas, as an enthusiastic Jacobite, refused to have anything to do with Queen Victoria, and would not handle paper money bearing her likeness.)

Lucas also welcomed children into the house at Great Wymondley, throwing a party for up to 200 of them every Good Friday when each of the young revellers would be presented with a penny, a penny bun and a glass of watered gin. Similar generosity was shown to Catholic callers (or perhaps that should be anyone who professed to be Catholic), presumably out of respect for his late mother who had been a follower of the Roman faith.

However, Lucas' lifestyle was by definition an injurious one and, in 1874, he died of a fit aged 60. His corpse, once washed and trimmed of surplus nails and hair, was according to contemporary reports, found to be as white and smooth as alabaster, and (having shooed out a family of foxes who had taken up residence elsewhere in the house) a team of labourers was soon hard at work removing some 17 cartloads of wood ash from the kitchen floor.

CHAPTER FIVE

Hoarders and Hobbyists

MARGARET FOUNTAINE (1862–1940)

Of broken hearts and butterfly wings

H ELL hast no fury like a woman scorned, but clearly once in a while that same energy can be put to a better use, which brings us to the case of Margaret Elizabeth Fountaine and her world-beating collection of butterflies.

Not of course that there is anything particularly unusual (let alone eccentric) about an English gentlewoman being in pursuit of her hobby and pacing the clipped lawn with a butterfly net in hand. It is just that this redoubtable Norfolk lass seems to have taken it to quite extraordinary extremes.

Spurned by her lover, an Irish cathedral chorister called Septimus Hewson who was eventually sacked for being drunk, young Margaret's response was to buy a cork helmet, a pair of plimsolls and a butterfly net and set sail for far shores. Initially she went to France and then Italy, where she pursued her flying beauties using a new-fangled device called a bicycle until she was chased by Corsican bandits and had to head for Hungary instead.

Pursued by one of the bandits – hence the scandal, for from then on this particular unmarried woman was rarely without the company of a foreign male and a bottle of brandy – Margaret was soon trekking through the ancient Magyar kingdom, often spending up to 12 hours a day on the move, sustained by little more than that brandy, coarse bread and ewe's milk.

Eventually she came to the Middle East, where she met a Greek Orthodox Syrian called Khalil Neimy aka 'Charles' – the Corsican had presumably returned home by now – who worked as a dragoman and remained her close companion for the next 28 years despite having a wife

back home in Damascus. Together, the two of them set off in search of yet more butterflies, Miss Fountaine first bathing in creosote to ward off leeches, and remained together long enough to visit more than 60 countries on six different continents.

Unsurprisingly, the two became experts in their field, and Margaret bred eggs from many of the tropical species she found. Thereafter, she was to build up an immense body of knowledge about butterfly life-cycles, all the while trying to come to terms with her own, somewhat complex emotional life.

Today recalled as much as a diarist as a lepidopterist, Miss Fountaine ordered that her journals remain sealed until 1978 (the centenary of her having started to compile the 12 large leather-bound volumes) when it was discovered that, for her, each year was taken as starting on 15 April rather than on 1 January. The diaries end with her death in 1940, of a heart attack on a Trinidadian mountainside, prior to which she sadly noted in the final volume that, 'the greatest passion, and perhaps the most noble love of my life was no doubt for Septimus Hewson, and the blow I received from his heartless conduct left a scar upon my heart, which no length of time ever quite effaced.'

With a staggering total of more than 22,000 different specimens to her name, Margaret Fountaine is these days commemorated at the Norwich

Castle Museum which now looks after the hugely impressive Fountaine-Neimy Collection.

JOHN STEWART (1749-1822)

I'd walk a million miles . . .

For John Stewart, life was all about walking and books, and whilst he had other odd aspects to his character – when in London he frequently dressed as an Armenian and sought out cows so he could inhale their exhalations – his most remarkable feats were definitely those which involved his feet.

Stewart was active in India where at various times he was an East India Company writer or clerk, an Indian Army general and the Nabob of Arcot's Prime Minister. When his time came to leave the subcontinent he decided to do it on foot. Taking in India, Turkey, Persia, the Middle East, Ethiopia, North Africa and most of the countries of Europe including frozen Lapland, the journey took him more than two decades during which time he learned an additional eight languages and formed his own, personal philosophy which he attempted to promote once he got back home.

He did this through a series of more than 30 books and pamphlets, many of which he gave away on the street whilst clothed in Armenian national dress. In 1790, he published his most famous work, *Travels over the most interesting parts of the Globe*, in which he attempted to explain the basic tenets of his new philosophy. Combining elements of pantheism, the thoughts of Spinoza and some traditional yogic notions of a single indissoluble consciousness, it was largely gobbledygook, although both William Wordsworth and Thomas de Quincey insisted its author was one of the most eloquent men of his age and nothing short of a genius.

Maybe the two Lakeland neighbours were joking – or perhaps they just gave up before getting to the bit where Stewart explained his theory of atomic transmutation whereby a man standing next to an animal automatically exchanges human body matter for that of the animal as the atoms on their respective surfaces mingle in the air. According to Stewart, this takes place at a rate of up to half a pound an hour, the worry being that before long the man would eventually become the beast, and vice versa.

Not that any of this actually bothered Stewart, though; far from it. In fact in later life his only real concern was that people should read his books and

continue doing so into the future for the benefit of successive generations. To start the ball rolling he planned to have his name carved in giant letters on Atlantic cliff faces (so that travellers would have their curiosity aroused and buy the books) and he employed De Quincey and others to translate everything he had written into Latin just in case the reading and writing of English went out of fashion.

His readers were also encouraged to find somewhere secure, bone-dry and preferably at least 8 ft underground in which to safeguard their own copies for future use. Stewart insisted they were to tell no-one where this secret place was, and then on their deathbed to pass the intelligence on only to the very closest and most trusted of friends.

De Quincey again took him at his word, apparently burying a set of Stewart volumes beneath his garden at Grasmere – but then he was a former junkie. In February 1822, reassured that the right things were being done to ensure his immortality, Stewart took laudanum and died quietly in a rented room close to Trafalgar Square. All his publications are of course now out of print.

CHARLES WATERTON (1782–1865)

The creature creator

With an interest in wildlife and the money to indulge it, Charles Waterton returned from his travels in South America where, having encountered such exotica as chameleons, lemurs, sunbirds and alligators, he conceived a plan to create what was perhaps the world's first ever nature reserve.

Waterton didn't call it that, of course, but having 'suffered and learnt mercy' whilst recovering from yellow fever he had become firmly opposed to the destruction of any wildlife. This itself was something of an eccentricity in an age when hunting, shooting and fishing were meat and drink to country squires such as he, but returning to Yorkshire (and keen to keep the wildlife in and the poachers out) Waterton spent a fortune building three miles of high stone wall around his Walton Hall estate.

The cost of this, some £9,000 (two or three million pounds in our own debased currency) Waterton claimed to have saved by giving up wine, and by eating little more than dry toast and watercress. After his wife died, he started to sleep on the floor as well (and for 35 years used a wooden block for a pillow) and was frequently seen walking around his park barefoot or sitting in tree tops reading Latin verse.

Keen to encourage wildlife to thrive, Waterton installed artificial nesting boxes – a world first and his own innovation – as well as importing rare owls from Italy in the hope they would breed. He also instructed his forester to leave any hollow logs or branches lying in the park to provide nesting places for lesser species.

Waterton took things further still inside the Hall with his collection of household pets including an albino hedgehog, a duck without the usual webbed feet, a species of toad collected in Brazil, and a three-toed sloth. Sometimes he would also pretend to be some species or other himself, dropping down onto all fours and nipping at visitors' ankles as they waited in the hall.

At one point, Waterton kept a vampire bat in his bedroom in the hope it would bite him so that he could write up the symptoms. But unfortunately, and despite his best efforts – he routinely slept with one temptingly unstockinged foot poking out from under the covers – the bat decided to bite a servant instead and the experiment was judged a failure.

Clearly Waterton's respect for these animals didn't extend as far as the grave, however, and whenever one of his rare pets died he would have it stuffed, mounted and put on display. Once he even dissected a gorilla on the dining room table before the port came round, and occasionally, if he felt the resulting pieces of taxidermy were insufficiently exotic, he would mix and match parts from many different animals in order to make up something of his own.

Examples of this included the 'Noctifer', which reportedly combined bits of an eagle owl with those from a bittern, the 'Nondescript' (a dried howler monkey which looked disturbingly like an Eskimo mummy) and something Waterton described as 'John Bull and the National Debt' with a vaguely human face applied to the body of a porcupine and half-concealed beneath the shell of a tortoise.

Unfortunately, Waterton's advanced ideas were not supported by his son – quite the reverse. Edmund Waterton held shooting parties in the park in the hope of paying off his debts and eventually Walton Hall was sold and the estate broken up. Today it's an hotel, and the Noctifer, the Nondescript and the rest of them were taken to Wakefield Museum. Waterton himself is still there, however, buried somewhere in the grounds between his two favourite trees.

WOGAN PHILLIPS, LORD MILFORD (1902-1993)

More a hobby-horse, perhaps, than a hobby

Wogan Phillips was hardly the first man to call for the abolition of the House of Lords, or for that matter the first person to describe it as 'an undemocratic anachronism composed of the inheritors of wealth and privilege bent on their protection [and] an indefensible obstacle to progressive legislation and the forward march of world socialism.'

He was, however, the first to mount such an attack from the red benches themselves, and in choosing to ignore the convention that maiden speeches in the Chamber avoid reference to controversial topics he did not seem to notice a certain irony in that it was only his own privileged position (as the first self-proclaimed Communist ever to sit in the Lords) that enabled him to launch the attack in the first place.

That said, whilst he relished the privilege, he never got his hands on the wealth. His father, the 1st Lord Milford, immediately disinherited him upon hearing that he had joined the Communist Party of Great Britain and refused to speak to him again. One of three brothers to be raised to the peerage through their own efforts (the others being Viscount St Davids (q.v.) and Lord Kylsant), Lord Milford was reluctant even to name his son in his will, and instead instructed the trustees to ensure that all interest in his estate be forfeited by any 'avowed Communist or fellow traveller with the Communist Party.'

As for the 2nd Lord Milford, he doesn't seem to have been all that bothered by this, dismissing his family as 'all very rich businessmen [and] so tremendously anti-semitic'. Declaring that he had no time for 'hunting, shooting, and all that,' he clearly wasn't too fond of the House of Lords either, noting that when he got there he had a tremendous welcome from all his old friends from Eton and Magdalen College, Oxford but that after he had made his speech 'no-one even offered me a drink'.

In the end it fell to Labour's Lord Attlee to offer the usual congratulations to the new Member on his speech, although even he could not resist observing that only in England could the views of the Communist Party be heard in the Lords, and 'that, of course, is an advantage of the hereditary principle'. Attlee was also kind enough not to refer to events in Stalin's Russia, although he presumably knew that despite his sabre-rattling, Milford privately acknowledged the USSR had turned out to be a complete disaster.

CHARLES BROOKING

Knobs and knockers . . . and so much more

With his collection now housed in the architecturally spectacular environment of London's University of Greenwich, Charles Brooking these days looks more like a visionary than an eccentric.

He single-mindedly set out to rescue endangered bits of domestic architecture whilst still a schoolboy, and in the process single-handedly invented the whole concept of architectural salvage. Indeed his collection is now the largest archive of original architectural features of its kind anywhere in Europe.

In fact, Brooking says he was only about three years old when he first became aware of architectural detailing, at that young age, he was already fascinated by the different font styles used for house-numbering on the doors of the street where he was growing up in Cheam. Within a year, he says, he switched to door handles before moving on again to the study of

window fixtures when he was only five or six. Soon, he was an inveterate collector of anything which would otherwise be thrown away and by his early teens he saw the need to specialise – not least, one suspects, to prevent his collections eventually squeezing his family out of the front door and onto the street.

It was doors and windows which caught his attention most – that and the associated fixtures and fittings which he continued to rescue wherever examples came under threat from skips, the wrecker's ball or terminal rot. He also grabbed anything not covered by other collections, such as fire grates, rainwater heads from downpipes, and on occasion even entire staircases.

Now more than 30 years on, there are some obvious gems among the 20,000 or so windows, doors, door knobs, fanlight sections and even boot scrapers which he has preserved, many dating back 500 years or more. These include items from the Royal Box at the old Wembley Stadium and from 10 Downing Street, a window retrieved from Windsor Castle, several more from Buckingham Palace and a sweeping fragment of balustrade from a house formerly owned by a member of The Who.

It is no surprise then that the huge collection features many of the big names in architecture such as Adam, Voysey and Lutyens. But Brooking is clearly no snob about this kind of thing and looking through the collection one is as likely to stumble upon scraps of dado or architrave from a suburban semi as a piece of more obviously grand or monumental architectural stone or metalwork.

Brooking says he realised long ago that he was 'possibly in danger of being labelled an eccentric. [But] I saw no reason to let that worry me'. Instead he busied himself, and continues to do so, preserving 'modest everyday features such as the humble ledged- and boarded or bead butt cottage front door, the Yorkshire light, or the 12-pane sash so often the victim of the restorers hand.' All are the sorts of things which are routinely ignored by mainstream museums which lack the time, resources, expertise and of course space to deal with this kind of material.

So good for Mr Brooking! If the individuals in this book share anything it must be the ability to withstand criticism or the pitying gaze of friends and strangers, and we've certainly seen time and again how much good can come out of this sort of refusal to toe the conventional line.

Certainly Brooking's legacy – with some justification he describes himself now as an architectural historian and consultant rather than a mere collector – will be a valued one with architects poring over items in the collection for decades to come; local historians and social archaeologists finding in the collection a myriad clues to the way we used to live, and of course others such as conservation officers referring to Brooking's collection to assist them with the historically accurate restoration of period homes and other buildings.

Quite an achievement, then, not that for me at any rate it does anything at all to offset the mind's-eye picture of a somewhat eccentric three year-old dragging his parents up and down the street looking at door numbers, counting knobs and checking out the knockers . . .

SIR HERVEY ELWES (d.1763) AND JOHN MEGGOT (1714–1789)

Inheriting the miser gene

A classic, storybook miser, Sir Hervey Elwes, Bart. of Stoke-by-Clare on the Essex-Suffolk border was, without doubt, among the richest men in Eighteenth Century England – with a fortune well in excess of £250,000.

He nevertheless made it his business to get by on no more than 110 guineas a year. This he did by paying his servants peanuts, wearing his great- and great-great grandfathers' clothes until they fell to pieces, and going to bed at dusk in order to save on candles. The fires would only very rarely be lit at his potentially splendid home, Stoke College (mostly Georgian, the house incorporates the surviving portions of an Eleventh Century Benedictine priory) with the Baronet preferring to keep warm by pacing up and down furiously, although he would, very occasionally, allow his guests one piece of kindling at a time.

Guests, mind you, were relatively rare, which was just as well since the only food offered them was some fish or partridge (all of it caught or shot on the estate) with a single boiled potato per person on the side. Needless to say, most guests would not willingly subject themselves to the experience more than once and, indeed, it seems that the only regular visitor was Sir Hervey's nephew, John Meggot, who used to travel down from London to see his uncle.

The son of a rich Southwark brewer who died when he was just three or four, Meggot was raised by his mother Amy Elwes Meggot. She starved to death in 1753 despite inheriting around £100,000 in property and bonds, but Meggot, initially at least, showed no signs of miserliness himself. On

the contrary, Westminster-educated and something of a scholar although he was never known to read a book once he had left school, Meggot spent some years enjoying the life of fashionable young man about town. He gambled until the early morning at Arthur's and the other leading clubs of St James's and once remained at the tables for two days and a night. He was also recognised by his friends as both a gourmand and an expert on wine.

These passions increased when Meggot inherited his mother's fortune, but when he visited his uncle in Suffolk he would undergo a startling trans-formation, stopping at Chelmsford to change into his shabbiest suit and taking the precaution of dining with a neighbour to prepare himself for his uncle's meagre fare. He would then present himself at Stoke as if his uncle's parsimonious way of living was the most natural thing in the world.

Meggot's attitude changed, however, when his uncle died in 1763. He inherited not just his uncle's estates and name but suddenly his disposition to meanness as well. Indeed John Elwes (as he now called himself) embarked on a life which in its particularities was even more bizarre than his uncle's had been.

Elwes put much of his money to good use and developed a series of magnificent townhouses in London's smarter quarters of Marylebone and St James's. At the same time, most of his business investments were seen as wise ones, and as well as restoring the stables and kennels at Stoke – to house a private pack of hounds and a superb collection of hunters – Elwes was elected to Parliament as the Member for Berkshire.

At Westminster, however, he rapidly gained a reputation as what the *Dictionary of National Biography* calls a 'political coquette' sitting on whichever side of the House felt right to him that day, and never making a single speech during the 12 years of his political career. At the same time, whilst known in London for his dandified appearance and voracious appetite, at his new home in Suffolk – where the indoor and outdoor staff totalled just one – he would typically sit down to nothing more than a bun although he once reportedly shared the corpse of a coot or moorhen with a rat. Similarly, and whereas he was happy to see a small fortune lavished on the best accommodation for his hounds and horses, Elwes was appar-ently wholly unconcerned at the sight of rainwater pouring through the ceilings of his home and reportedly never spent so much as a penny on what was already an old and extremely rundown place.

His eccentricities continued into his personal life too, so that he never married (despite fathering two sons on his housekeeper) and refused ever to have his shoes polished lest this wear out the leather prematurely. Instead he resorted to the trunk of his benefactor's great-great grandfather for clothes, and once donned a wig discarded in a hedge by a tramp. On top of this, he wore a hat stolen from a scarecrow.

Elwes would also ride his horses on the grass verge (to extend the life of horseshoes) as he journeyed between his Suffolk property and his London ones. And he frequently undertook the most enormous detours if this would enable him to avoid paying turnpike tolls. Finally, when he got to town, he would sleep semi-rough in whichever of his many properties was unlet rather than fitting one out for himself and, in all his life, he never acquired much in the way of furniture, preferring instead to drag pieces from one room to the next if and when they were required.

Elwes' memory began to test him in old age and the occasional bad investment is said to have cost him an incredible £250,000. Even so, his will dated 1786 mentions property totalling half a million pounds and, when he died some three years later, his nephew and two illegitimate sons shared around £800,000.

JOHN CAMDEN NEILD (1780-1852)

Chelsea pensioner extraordinaire

Like Meggot and Elwes, John Camden Neild believed that spending money was not the thing to do, and like Meggot he realised this only after coming into his inheritance.

He inherited around a quarter of a million pounds, but that was about all since there was nothing in his genetic makeup to match that of his father's, a kindly prison reformer and philanthropist on a substantial scale. Neild Jnr., a barrister, much preferred to hoard his cash with (in the words of his biographer) 'avarice being his ruling passion and for the last 30 years of his life he was entirely given over to the accumulation of wealth'.

Unlike the other misers described here, Neild preferred London to a rundown country pile, and owned a large house on the Thames at Cheyne Walk, Chelsea. He slept on the floor for much of his life, however, only ever occupying a single room. He thought clothes were a complete waste of money, and on the occasions when he ventured out he typically wore Eighteenth Century leftovers which he refused to brush or clean on the grounds that this would simply wear them out. Neild refused to pay for an overcoat and, in bad weather, would protect himself with an old green cotton parasol.

Neild also owned substantial properties in Middlesex, Kent, Surrey and Buckinghamshire and, rather than pay an agent, preferred to collect the rents himself frequently travelling out to the country on the back of a wagon to avoid paying the fare. On the rare occasions when he was forced to travel on a coach, he would select the cheapest seat outside on the roof, and remain there at the halts rather than paying over yet more money each time the coach stopped at an inn. Similarly, if Neild's business required him to stay a night or two in the country he would prevail upon one of his tenants to give him free bed and board.

In contrast, Neild once gave a sovereign to a local school close to one of his estates, contributed annually to appeals from the London Asylum for the Blind, and even paid for the schooling of a tenant's exceptionally bright son. But this was far from the norm, and it certainly didn't indicate a permanent change in his ways.

For instance, when it was time for Neild to repair the roof of North Marston church which he was obliged to do as the owner of the living, he instructed the workmen to use calico and canvas in place of lead. He told them to paint it with tar in the hope that this botch of a job would see out his time and he sat up on the roof all day to make sure that nobody attempted to steal the materials he'd so generously funded.

Eventually, Neild was laid to rest in the church too, and today it looks pretty chipper thanks to its later benefactor, Queen Victoria, who put up a stained glass window at the east end of the building. This she did in memory of the Chelsea miser, not because they were friends –they never met – but because, when his will was read in 1852, it transpired that he had left almost his entire fortune to the Queen 'begging for Her Majesty's most gracious acceptance of the same, for her sole use and benefit, and her heirs, &c'.

It wasn't quite the sort of philanthropy his father would have recognised, but as the sum involved is thought to have been about £25 million in today's terms, the Queen's purchase shortly afterwards of Balmoral may not be entirely unconnected to the strange case of John Camden Neild.

SIR THOMAS BARRETT-LENNARD (1826–1918)

Four legs good . . .

Born in 1826, Thomas Barrett-Lennard took an M.A. at Peterhouse, Cambridge, succeeded to his grandfather's baronetcy at the age of 31 and, as a traditional local Victorian grandee, held the offices of High Sheriff of Essex (and later of County Monaghan), of Justice of the Peace for Essex, and of Deputy Lieutenant of the same county where as chairman of the County's Asylums Committee he was charged with the care of the rest of the local loons.

What mostly interested him, however, were his animals which he held in the highest esteem, his fondness for four-legged creatures extending not just to the usual retinue of horses, hounds and pointers which would have been found around any English country home at this time, but also to the many rats which ran in the fields and barns of his gloriously Gothic estate, Belhus in Essex.

The family horses, dogs and cats were buried in special plots in the grounds when their time was up, this sort of pet cemetery being common-place on big estates in the years before the Great War. But Sir Thomas

took things a good deal further than most, insisting not only that the vicar from nearby Aveley officiate at the proceedings but also that his own footmen attend in full livery and take the weight of the animals' caskets which were purpose-made for the occasion.

Whether the rats got the same treatment at Belhus is not recorded, although they certainly had a better time than most, with Sir Thomas insisting the outdoor staff ensure that bowls of fresh water were provided for them in the haybarns and expressly forbidding anyone on the staff to kill or injure a rodent found within the house or grounds.

The result, unsurprisingly, was that the rats thrived and (like those living in the Great War trenches) soon grew to such a size that, as one housemaid later put it, 'they were as big as cats, and as tame as tame could be. The noise they made was like people running up and down the corridor. Sometimes you could hear chairs moving – they were everywhere.' Rooks were another favourite.

Sir Thomas also refused to allow the deer at Belhus to be converted into venison and, although he was a member of the South Essex Hunt, he refused to ride with them, preferring to go steeplechasing rather than killing foxes. Otherwise kind enough to open his own front door to save the servants the bother, he nevertheless once administered a severe hiding to a tradesman whom he had caught mistreating a pony.

Sir Thomas was also a shabby dresser who, on more than one occasion, was mistaken for his own gatekeeper, and once, in later life, was apprehended on his way home from a meeting at a local asylum after the arresting officer made the understandable mistake of assuming that he was an escapee.

LIONEL WALTER, LORD ROTHSCHILD (1868-1937)

Putting the cart before the zebra

On one hand a zoologist with an international reputation, and an acknowledged expert in the collecting and taxonomy of birds and butterflies, the 2nd Lord Rothschild, known as Walter, was also the sort of man who entertained his dogs to dinner, trained a quartet of zebras to pull a variety of different carriages, lived with his mother for all but three years of his life and, on more than one occasion, was photographed riding a giant tortoise whilst encouraging the beast to move by waving a cabbage leaf a few inches ahead of its nose.

Educated at Cambridge before being employed (reluctantly) in the family bank, Rothschild's life-long interest in zoology was encouraged by a meeting with German-born zoologist Albrecht Karl Ludwig Gotthilf Günther, although his interest in collecting was already such that, by the age of just 13, his parents had taken the decision to employ a full-time assistant to help him catalogue his specimens. Upon reaching adulthood, he embraced his passion fully and began the long process of transforming his home at Tring Park, Hertfordshire into something of a private zoological museum. So impressive was the end result, that he was able to give his extensive purpose-built premises to the nation and their contents to the British Museum.

Never one to do things by halves – the collection of specimens is almost certainly the largest of its sort in the world, even though at one point he was forced to sell an incredible 295,000 stuffed birds to pay off a titled, female blackmailer – Rothschild's speciality was the painstaking, systematic classification of the various different species.

The only practical way to achieve this, he knew, was to build up his own collection (by this time, the Rothschild family as a whole were known to exhibit something of a mania for collecting) and this he duly did before

bringing the formidable powers of his computer-like brain to bear on the not inconsiderable problems of differentiating between the one species and another.

Working at this sort of thing for up to 14 hours a day, Rothschild and his staff produced literally millions of words of documentation to support their work, with Tring's in-house journal eventually extending to more than forty bound volumes. All the while, his Lordship and the team sat surrounded by more than 2,000 stuffed mammals, including every type of zebra known to man, 2,400 stuffed birds, 300 dried reptiles, 640 other reptiles, 200 mounted heads, 300 pairs of antlers, 1,400 animal skins and skulls, 300,000 bird skins, more than 300,000 beetles, 200,000 birds' eggs and an incredible 2.25 million different insects.

Needless to say, seekers after the curious would not have come away from Tring dissatisfied, since the collection also included several extinct species such as the quagga, the thylacine, a great auk, the giant sloth, a moa and a dodo. There was also a preserved specimen of a young zebroid, a stripey hybrid horse which had been bred by the great man himself.

Best of all, at least for our purposes, and despite his intelligence, Lord Rothschild never settled down to be normal. Thus, on one occasion as the Member for Aylesbury, he outraged the Commons by taking his seat wearing a white top hat. On another occasion, he drove his carriage and four-in-hand down the Mall and into the courtyard of Buckingham Palace – the four in this case being zebra. Although shy with women, Rothschild took absolutely no care to keep his assignations with actresses and young socialites secret – except from his mother – hence the aforementioned blackmailing incident. Finally, he is also the only person in this book to have a species of giraffe named after him, the five-horned Rothschild or Baringo Giraffe, *Giraffa camelopardalis rothschildi.*

HENRY CONSTANTINE JENNINGS
(1731–1819)

The original mad dog

Whilst Lord Rothschild was a reluctant banker, the family business at least saved him from the fate suffered by poor old Henry Constantine Jennings.

As avid a collector as Walter, but with an arguably much wider range of interests, Jennings seemingly collected anything and everything, from sea-

shells to statues, pictures to prints, and stuffed-birds to . . . er, creditors. The simple truth was that all too often, Jennings' possessions were obtained at the expense of somebody other than himself.

By no means a rich man but quite unable to control his acquisition mania, Jenning's desire to possess nearly everything he saw that was old or beautiful repeatedly landed the Oxfordshire-born antiquarian in trouble with a variety of different creditors. This led him to the debtors' court, and eventually the debtors' gaol as well when his other passion, high stakes gambling, really got a grip.

A partial solution to the problem came in 1816 when Jennings was once again consigned to a cell and decided to remain there with the choicest pieces of his collection rather than seeking to be free. Unfortunately, the cramped surroundings of a cell full to the rafters with antiques made for other problems. In particular, it made it difficult for him to stick to his punishing fitness regime – he had a horror of growing old and feeble – as this required him to wield a heavy steel broadsword 300 times a day on an artificial horse of his own devising ('composed of leather and inflated by wind like a pair of bellows') whilst galloping precisely 1,000 paces, never less and never more.

Needless to say, eventually, some of Jennings' treasures had to go, the most famous of them being his cherished 'Dog of Alcibiades' – named after a celebrated Fourth-Century Athenian – but these days better known to visitors to the British Museum as the Jennings Dog. Jennings was up to his eyes in gambling debts by 1778 and was not sorry to see it go, but when it raised a handsome 1,000 guineas at auction he was quick to comment, 'A fine dog it was, and a lucky dog was I to purchase it'. From then on, he was known around clubland as 'Dog' Jennings, a name which stuck.

The dog in question is one of only a very small number of Hellenistic animal sculptures and was copied in marble in the Roman period from a bronze original. It depicts the molossian, an ancestor of the modern mastiff which was native to Epirus and it is thought that, before the city was sacked by Rome in 168 B.C. the original bronze would have formed part of an important civic monument.

Jennings himself acquired it during a stay in Rome in the early 1750s, believing it to be the dog described in Plutarch who had a particularly attractive tail before it was docked by his owner. Better to give the Athenians something to talk about, argued Alcibiades, than to have them talk about himself. Upon its sale to Charles Duncombe, at whose Yorkshire estate it remained until 2001, Edmund Burke is said to have remarked that no dog was worth 1,000 guineas. To this, Dr. Johnson characteristically replied, 'Sir, it is not the worth of the thing, but the skill in forming it, which is so highly estimated.'

For many years, simply to have a copy of the work was enough to mark out a man as a gentleman of taste and, today, miniature copies are still to be found in garden centres up and down the country. Happily, when the time came for Duncombe's descendents to sell the great hound – by now the estate had come down to the Earls of Feversham – a temporary export ban was introduced giving the British Museum time to raise the necessary £662,297 to buy the sculpture which was eventually installed in the recently restored Great Court.

VICTORIA-JOSEFA DOLORES CATALINA, LADY SACKVILLE (1862–1936)

Charity begins at home

It's not hard to guess how the chippy, snobbish Vita Sackville-West would have reacted to the thought of her precious Sissinghurst Castle being thrown open to the public because, to her, the great unwashed were 'the bungaloid masses' – but her mother is a more difficult character to assess.

Certainly, her combination of Latin passion and Anglo-Saxon reserve would have marked her out from the crowd, for Lady Sackville was the result of an illicit affair between a Spanish dancer called Pepita and an English diplomat. But mostly it was her relationship with money which stands out today, with Victoria-Josefa demonstrating on the one hand a complete lack of understanding about its true value – for example, leaving a £10,000 cheque made out to cash in the back of a cab – and on the other, showing such incredible meanness as to spend an entire afternoon cutting up old postage stamps in order to save a few pennies by sticking the unfranked portions back together again and re-using them the following morning.

Certainly, it was this side of her which drove her own collecting. Thus, the franked portions of stamps would eventually find their way to her great medieval house Knole, where they would be stuck up in place of wallpaper. The desk drawers at the house would likewise be stuffed with headed paper pinched from hotels, whilst toilet rolls lifted from the ladies' room at Harrods would be used as stationery. It goes without saying that she wasn't one to waste money on coal or firewood either. On the contrary, the wind fairly whipped through Knole as Lady Sackville insisted the

doors and windows were pinned open even in the winter. In place of a scarf, she used an old pair of socks reputed to have once belonged to the architect Sir Edwin Lutyens.

Curiously for one with such a celebrated gardener as Vita for a daughter, Lady Sackville preferred porcelain and metal flowers to real ones, and once decorated her garden with coloured velvet and sequinned paper in place of anything more conventional. Fortunately, the staff mostly took such peccadilloes for granted, although more than once they quit *en masse* when her Ladyship went too far. On another occasion, an old nanny who had been in service with the family for many years was fired after being accused of stealing and consuming several dozen quail in a single sitting.

Like many a miser, Lady Sackville also worried constantly about money and her perceived lack of it. During the Great War, this led her to write to Lord Kitchener about her husband (asking that the 3rd Baron not be sent anywhere dangerous) not because she loved him but because the family would never be able to pay the death duty if he succumbed to something awful whilst in the trenches.

She wasn't above begging for money either and, while on occasions this was for others less fortunate than herself, it is generally now recognised that as her Ladyship was never quite able to distinguish between charity and racketeering, the chances are that most of the money sent to her at Knole in all likelihood probably stayed there.

This view is firmly reinforced by the fact that none of the Charity Commissioners had ever actually heard of Lady Sackville's Homeless Sleeping on Brighton Beach charity – sole officer and trustee: Lady Sackville – or one imagines, of the Roof of Friendship Fund which she set up a few years later in 1928. That she became so cross when one of those she approached gave her a tile instead of actual cash also lends credit to the notion that the roof in question was the leaky one at Knole rather than some larger, more spiritual organisation dedicated to bringing people closer together.

It's also worth mentioning that Lady Sackville could show considerable ingenuity too – or perhaps that should just be *chutzpah* – in the way she went about relieving others of their small change. For example, she set up what she called the Million Penny Fund in an attempt to clear the National Debt. To help the fund along, she intended to obtain a 'penny-for-every-year' from anyone whose birthday was mentioned in the newspaper and to this end would write to the relevant people asking them to return to her a penny for every year they had been alive. She also insisted they send her *three* stamped addressed envelopes with the money: one to refund to her the cost of the original begging letter, another to enable her to write to say thank you for the donation . . . and a third 'for a fresh victim'.

It's not known how much the Million Penny Fund raised in the end, but readers will know that the National Debt is with us still and has never been higher.

ECCENTRIC ROYAL ATTRIBUTES

- Elizabeth I was the first monarch to have her own toilet.
- George IV is the only royal to have employed prize fighters as bouncers at his coronation. On his wedding night, he insisted Caroline of Brunswick smoke a pipe in bed.
- George VI liked to run cine films backwards and never tired of watching swimmers exit the pool feet first so as to end up on the diving board.
- A keen card-player, Queen Victoria insisted that anyone who lost to her pay up immediately using only newly-minted coins. She was good at cards too, meaning a supply had to be kept at the Palace for this purpose. The same monarch later replaced all the palace loo rolls with newspaper as an economy measure.
- George V was the first monarch ever to go down a coalmine. He also insisted alcohol be banned from all royal households for the duration of the Great War – although he kept back a regular supply for himself.
- Edward VII had an American-style bowling alley installed at Sandringham, liked to have three washbasins for his own use – one each for hands, face and teeth – and so much enjoyed watching buildings on fire that he had his own fireman's uniform made in order that he could do so without being identified.
- George III's son, Augustus, Duke of Sussex, possessed more than 5,000 copies of The Bible. His mother was the last royal to boast an official court dwarf.
- Princess Anne was the first Royal to qualify for a Heavy Goods Vehicle licence and can legally drive a lorry.

- Prince Charles is the first heir to the throne to have ridden a killer whale – and somewhat more surprisingly, the first in 300 years to have married an English girl (or two).
- When he travels through Scotland, the Prince is more correctly known as the Duke of Rothesay. As Duke of Cornwall, he owns Dartmoor Prison and is entitled to claim the cargo of any ship wrecked off the Cornish coast.
- Prince Philip has a special top-hat with a built-in radio so that he can catch up with the cricket score when racing with the Queen. For a while, he was also in the habit of barbecuing his own breakfast until HM objected to the smell.
- Edward VI kept a genuine whipping boy, Barnaby Fitzpatrick, who was beaten if the young king made a mistake in his lessons.
- Edward VIII, as Prince of Wales, enjoyed pronouncing certain words with a 'mockney' accent in order to annoy his father.
- Retaining an ancient right, the Queen can still, in theory, legally sell off the ships of the Royal Navy and disband the Army.

CHAPTER SIX

UFOs, Faddists and Flat-Earthers

WILLIAM FRANCIS BRINSLEY LE POER TRENCH, EARL OF CLANCARTY (1911–1995)

A FORMER advertising salesman for a gardening magazine and with a passion for flying saucers, Le Poer Trench is distinguished from your average UFO-loon by virtue of his seat in the House of Lords. As the 8th Earl of Clancarty and Marquess van Heusden in the Netherlands, he took advantage of his position to form the first official Parliamentary All-Party UFO Study Group. He did this in order to assist him in his lifelong bid to prove his theory that the majority of unidentified flying objects arrive here not from outer space but from secret bases located deep inside the Earth which (he insisted) is actually hollow.

According to Lord Clancarty, who also founded and edited the pioneering *Flying Saucer Review*, countless aliens are among us and frequently kidnap human beings in order to brainwash them. Following this procedure, they are returned to the 'Upper Earth' (through a series of seven or eight tunnels) where they continue living as programmed agents.

Clancarty was candid enough to admit that, 'I haven't been down there myself but from what I gather [these beings] are very advanced.' To substantiate his theory, he produced a series of genuine satellite photographs showing what he firmly maintained were large tunnel entrances at both the North and South Poles. He also wrote a number of books on the subject, all of which are unsurprisingly long out of print.

The likes of *Burke's Peerage* and *Who's Who* show him to have been the fifth son of the 5th Earl of Clancarty, and to have succeeded his half-brother, Grenville Sydney Rochefort. But for his part, Clancarty preferred

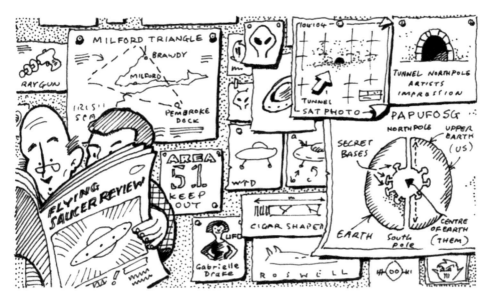

to look rather further back and, at one point, claimed to have traced his own family tree back to around 63,000 B.C. which was approximately the time when the beings first arrived to colonise the interior of our planet. Sadly, that long pedigree came to a sudden full stop when the Earl died childless, in 1995, despite having been married four times.

ADAM ISMAIL

Part-Time Martian

In July 1997, the *Daily Telegraph* reported that Mr Ismail and two friends, Mustafa Khalil and Abdullah al-Umari, had filed a lawsuit against NASA after the latter had sent its first Pathfinder spacecraft and Sojourner rover to Mars without first seeking their express permission.

Claiming ownership of the red planet – on the grounds that the Yemeni-born trio had inherited all rights to the whole caboodle from their ancestors who inhabited the planet more than 3,000 years ago – the three men attempted to prevent the US space agency from publicising any further details of conditions on Mars until the case had come to court.

Documents substantiating their case were said to have been lodged with the Yemeni prosecutor-general in San'a, and Ismail and his colleagues gave an interview to the Arabic-language paper *Al-Thawri* insisting that the planet was theirs.

For its part, however, NASA showed no signs of slowing or cancelling its projected Mars mission, with the organisation's news chief, Brian Welch, instead dismissing the case as 'a ridiculous claim. Mars is a planet out in the solar system that is the property of all humanity, not just two or three guys in the Yemen.' He said he too had paperwork to support his position, pointing out that a 1967 international treaty holds that everything in the solar system, except Earth itself, 'is the property of everyone in the world and no one country.'

THOMAS DAY (1748-1789)

Perfect man seeks perfect woman

Whilst he was shrewd enough to recognise that 'a lawyer is more noxious to most people than a spider' Thomas Day, himself a lawyer, had a few theories which, were he to put them into practice today, would doubtless have seen him locked up.

In particular, he had a thing about finding a wife who would see things his way, and when he failed to do this set out to create one in his own image. His starting point was to adopt a couple of 12 year-old orphans, Sabrina and Lucretia, the idea being to raise them and train them to see life as he did and to want to live as he planned to live.

He wasn't a complete rogue, however, and had a document drawn up in which he promised to defend their honour – from himself, presumably – and to make some financial reparations to whichever of the duo failed to make the grade (at which point she would be cast out when he went off to marry the other).

Once the paperwork was in order, he took the pair to Avignon in France, which he felt was far enough away from the influence of England and the English. There he settled down to teach his two (hopefully) noble savages from scratch, educating them in science, literature and moral philosophy.

Strangely, the experiment failed and, when the two teenage girls began to fight among themselves, the trio returned to England where he paid off

Lucretia – the stupider of the two, he thought – before setting up home in the Midlands with Sabrina.

But sadly she too soon fell short of his expectations, refusing to read the books he chose for her and insisting on screaming when he dripped hot wax on her arms rather than bearing the pain with his own brand of heroic fortitude. Accordingly, she too was packed off – to boarding school – after which, somewhat frustratingly for Day, she married the lawyer who had drawn up her official adoption documents before the trio had first set sail for France.

Day meanwhile turned to his neighbour, and when she rejected him, to her younger sister who was at least kind enough to explain that with his weird theories and scruffy demeanour he was no kind of a catch for a lady with aspirations.

Day's response was characteristically bizarre and, rather than just buying some new clothes and dropping a few of his stranger ideas, he returned to France where he spent a full year learning to fence, dance, converse in a civilised fashion, and to stand more upright. For the latter he would spend hours in a wooden frame constructed for this purpose, but upon his return, he was quickly rejected once again on the grounds that he'd now made himself look ridiculous whereas before he'd just been plain weird.

Determined to leave women well alone from now on, he travelled to London, and promptly fell in love with one called Esther Milnes. Possessed of a large fortune and a good brain, she nevertheless welcomed the chance to live the kind of simple, spartan life Day had been proposing for all these years, and things began to look up.

After marrying in 1778, the two of them bought a farm in Essex, deliberately choosing a broken down one with poor soil in the belief that they had no right to luxuries whilst the poor wanted bread. For three years, they stuck at it too, working themselves silly and sleeping in a windowless cell, before eventually admitting defeat and buying a better one.

They gave away the rest of Esther's fortune and when Day suddenly died (believing horses would respond to kindness rather than formal training, he had been thrown to his death) Esther, clearly bereft, chose to live in total darkness. Refusing to get up except at night, she followed him to the grave in 1791.

JAMES BURNETT, LORD MONBODDO
(1714–1799)

She cut off their tails with a carving knife . . .

Said to be 'By far the most learned judge of his time' and by common repute, one of the most respected and eminent of them to sit at the Edinburgh Court of Sessions, Lord Monboddo is nevertheless a chap remembered as much for his odd opinions as for his sound judgements. When you hear them, it's not hard to see why.

Anything modern was a waste of time as far as his Lordship was concerned and, if the Ancient Greeks didn't need it, and didn't use it, neither did he. Coaches were out then, also sedan-chairs – although he would allow his wig to travel in one on its way to court whilst Monboddo himself travelled everywhere by horse.

Unfortunately, the same logic allowed him to defend slavery; Plutarch had, and that was reason enough for Monboddo. Until his death he also failed to understand why a man of Johnson's ability would waste it compiling a dictionary of English when Ancient Greek was so much the better tongue.

Monboddo wouldn't sit with his fellow judges on the Bench either, preferring for personal reasons to sit down in the body of the court with his clerks. But best of all he insisted that orangutans were really men, and that men were really monkeys, a fact concealed by a conspiracy of midwives who cut off the tails of every new born baby before allowing the mother to see it.

He was serious too, in 1773 publishing his 'proof' in a volume called *Of the Origin and Progress of Language* which contained evidence that the famous orange apes were also capable of speech, and which pointed to the Bay of Bengal as the likely place from which these humans with tails had first sprung.

Thereafter, it remained a source of great frustration to him that, despite observing firsthand the births of all his own children, Monboddo had, on each occasion, been outwitted by the midwife and failed to see the knife or the evidence of its usage. Consequently, he was eventually forced to abandon this part of his theory, although by then the wags knew his name and today his reputation as an important early evolutionary theorist still suffers badly as a result.

In 1785, when he was 71, very deaf and extremely short-sighted, Monboddo was visiting London and the Court of the King's Bench when a rumour started that the building was caving in. As the other judges, plaintiffs and witnesses clambered over each other in an attempt to get out, Lord Monboddo remained calm and in his place and refused to move at all.

In the end it proved to be a false alarm, and when asked why he too hadn't attempted to flee the building Monboddo insisted that he had assumed that it was all part of normal court proceedings south of the border. A sudden, strangely violent but presumably traditional ceremony which as a stranger to English Law he had no way of comprehending.

CHARLES KAY OGDEN
(1889-1957)

Back to basics

All of us do things at University which, when revisited as an adult, might cause us to shudder with embarrassment. Even so, one suspects that

Charles Kay Ogden was probably the only man during his time at Cambridge to draw attention to himself by smoking a pretend cigarette.

Equipped with a tiny red bulb at one end in order that it might glow authentically, the item in question was believed by its user to have some strange health-giving properties. Ogden reached the conclusion somewhere that fresh air was harmful and decided that whenever he was indoors all the windows must be locked shut. To compensate for this he carted around what he called an 'ozone machine', insisting that it produced air of an altogether higher calibre than that which was circulating outside. He also kept a coffin at home, just in case he was wrong.

It was at this time too that he started collecting books and incunabula by the roomful, his collections being sufficiently impressive that on his death they were acquired by University College London and UCLA. He was also strangely secretive despite being highly sociable, and so singularly possessive of his friends that he tried to keep different groups of them in separate compartments and would become highly agitated if anybody from one compartment somehow gained access to somebody from another.

Something of a linguist, philosopher, writer and publisher – during the Great War he got around paper shortages by pulping old comics to produce his firmly anti-establishment *Cambridge Magazine* – Ogden also founded the Orthological Institute in a bid to promote a new invention of his, something which he called 'Basic English'.

With a total vocabulary of only 850 words it was certainly basic, comparing more than a little unfavourably with the vocab of the average university graduate – thought to have an active repertoire of 60,000 words, and a passive vocabulary of 75,000 more – and frankly sounded like a complete non-starter when measured against standard, spoken English with its more than half a million entries in the *Oxford English Dictionary*.

Winston Churchill liked it, however, and in 1943 as its most famous champion, he went so far as to propose in a speech to the faculty at Harvard that B.E. be adopted internationally with all possible speed. The British Government liked it too (despite its creator's antagonism towards the authorities) seeing in it a possibly valuable tool in securing world peace through multi-party negotiation, and it supported the initiative financially for more than a decade.

The trouble was that Ogden was just about the worst promoter imagi-nable. He had a thing about masks, for one thing. He had scores of different ones and every time a journalist or academic came to interview him about his new language he quickly fell into the habit of nipping out of the room every few minutes and coming back in wearing yet another mask. He'd do the same with Government officials and Civil Servants too, and indeed seemed so bent on thwarting his own progress that, at one point, he went so far as to insist that the local telephone exchange no longer put through calls from the Chairman of the Cabinet Committee on Basic English.

Eventually, officialdom had had enough of this. Who could blame them? Basic English conked out, the events leading to its ultimate demise being no better described than in Ogden's own self-penned entry in *Who's Who*: 'Career – 1946–8 – bedevilled by officials.'

SIR THOMAS URQUHART (1611–1660)

Crouting, gueriating and curking

Just as John Bigg (q.v.) fell to pieces following Charles II's restoration to the throne, Sir Thomas is said to have died laughing with joy, having waited so long for the happy return of his horse-loving monarch and then literally fallen at the final hurdle.

A good royalist through and through – Charles I had knighted him in

1641 – Urquhart fell on hard times during the Commonwealth, spending time in the Tower at the Protector's pleasure, having his possessions seized upon his release, and then spending the next several years appealing to the authorities for their return.

Like Charles Kay Ogden he had a thing about language too, but where Ogden's approach to the creation of a universal language was designed to be simple enough for a child to grasp, Urquhart's 'trigonometrical treatise' *Trissotetras* is no easier to understand now that it was when it first appeared in 1644. Instead, delighting in the obscure, the recondite and the arcane – and describing them in a language so dense as to be almost Urquhart's own – the finished work is something which even the erudite compilers of *Encyclopaedia Britannica* felt compelled to describe as 'almost impenetrably obscure'.

This remains so even though Urquhart included an extensive glossary explaining at length the meanings of some of the more singular of the terms he chose to employ such as 'amfractuosities' and 'cathetobasall'. The first of these is apparently a reference to 'the cranklings, windings, turnings and involutions belonging to the equisoleary Scheme' whilst the latter (according to Urquhart) 'is said of the Concordance of Loxo-gononspshericall Moods, in the Datas of the Perpendicular, and the Base, for finding out of the Maine question.'

See? Clear as mud. Part of the problem, perhaps, was that Urquhart just took on too much at the one time. Simultaneously tracing his own ancestry back 143 generations – going right back to the 'red earth' from which divine hands had wrought Adam – he claimed to have discovered Pamprosodos Urquhart, son-in-law to the Pharaoh and the chap whose wife rescued Moses from the Nile.

His studies in this direction had doubtless fed into his new language too it was a new tongue which he insisted had precisely 66 advantages over all those languages then current, advantages which were said to include the use of 11 different genders, ten separate tenses and seven distinct moods.

Unfortunately, he refused to publish any more details about it, and said he would not do so until his property was returned and his parole conditions lifted. This never happened and he died abroad a relatively poor man, leaving us with only the tiniest fragments of his new language, most of which refer to the sounds animals make rather than human beings. For the record though, they are as follows: nuzzing (camel) boing (buffalo) coniating (stork) smuttering (monkey) curking (quail) and drintling (turkeys). Oh yes, I nearly forgot: beagles don't bark on Planet Urquhart, they 'charm'.

SIR TATTON SYKES (1826–1913)

No hot-head

For His Grace the Duke of Portland (q.v.) sporting several coats at a time and wearing a 2-ft black hat was a means of disguise. He failed to realise that no other man in England was at that time thus adorned. For Sir Tatton Sykes, however, the extra layers were more about maintaining a stable local environment, as for him there was no safer route to good health than ensuring that one's body remained at a constant temperature. To this end, he always went out wearing several overcoats that he could shed them one by one as the day progressed without allowing himself to get overheated or too cool for comfort.

He took this pet theory dead seriously too, going so far as to have the coats made in a number of different colours and sizes, each being large enough to fit comfortably over the preceding one, and with a similar arrangement for his trousers. In order to cool down extra quickly, he was also known to take off his shoes and socks before sticking his feet out of his carriage window as it went along.

To prevent him having to carry the items he discarded – he was a Yorkshire grandee, after all – he had an ongoing arrangement with local juveniles that anyone returning a coat or a pair of trousers to the kitchens at Sledmere would be rewarded with a shilling and a hot meal. In that way, he was free to drop his clothes where and whenever he felt like, shedding layers as he went whilst being reasonably sure the items would eventually find their way home.

Like Lady Sackville at Knole (q.v.) he had no time for flowers either, calling them 'nasty, untidy things', and as well as ploughing up the beds and lawns on his own estate, would use his cane to behead any he found growing in the village. When a tenant asked to grow some flowers, Sir Tatton insisted they be cauliflowers, and he also instigated a bylaw barring tenants from using their front doors which he preferred to be locked in order to prevent misuse.

Later, as his mania for this sort of thing progressed, he had a number of houses on the estate designed with painted *trompe l'oeil* entrances instead of real ones, thereby forcing those who were housed in them to get in and out round the back. It is however notable that when the big house at

Sledmere was rebuilt (it burned down in 1911), Sir Tatton refused to leave until he had finished eating his pudding – he was a great one for puddings – and then had the architect fit up his own house with a large and functional front door which he went on to use.

THE ECCENTRIC AS A CONMAN

- The Marquess Montmorenci (1848–1911) was an improbably-named racehorse tipster whose real name was Harry Benson and who amassed a fortune by tipping imaginary horses and bribing senior Scotland Yard officers to keep a step or two ahead of the law. Events caught up with him in the end, however, and after serving part of a sentence of 15 years' hard labour he fled to the US, restarted his dodgy dealings and eventually died in New York's Tombs Prison.
- Jonathan Wild (1689–1725) was London's self-styled Thief-taker General who made a mint returning stolen property to its rightful owners and claiming the rewards. Unfortunately, most of it he'd stolen himself, or paid others to do it for him and, after attempting to kill himself with laudanum, he was hanged at Tyburn before a cheering crowd of thousands.
- Dr William Dodd (1729–1777) was founder of the Humane Society for the Relief and Discharge of Small Debtors but turned out to be quite a big debtor himself. He forged a cheque drawn on the account of Lord Chesterfield for the then gigantic sum of £4,200, was found guilty at Newgate and executed next door.
- Lord Gordon-Gordon (1815–73) swindled a London jeweller out of £25,000 and railway entrepreneur Jay Gould out of an incredible one million bucks. Gordon-Gordon was eventually caught, jumped bail and fled to Canada in 1873. Frustrated in their attempts to extradite him, five of his dupes, including two future State Governors, and three future Congressman, tried to kidnap him and ended up in gaol themselves. Gordon-Gordon promptly threw a huge party to celebrate, sent his guests home with generous gifts and then

shot himself dead. More than a century later, his true identity has never been revealed.

- Michael Corrigan (1881–1946) appeared to be an impeccably respectable major in the Brigade of Guards but sold the Tower of London to a stranger, London Bridge at least twice, and the Duke of York's Piccadilly mansion to some credulous American tourists. He was arrested at the Ritz and, when found guilty, hanged himself in gaol – with his regimental tie, *naturellement*.

CHAPTER SEVEN

The Foodies

FRANCIS BUCKLAND (1826–1880)

Like father like son

THERE was clearly something in Buckland's genes (see his father, overleaf) but whereas your average gastronomic weirdo contents himself with formulating his own strange diet, Francis Trevelyan Buckland wanted everyone else to follow suit as well. To achieve this, he founded a dining club dedicated to persuading others to eat what he personally thought wholesome and sensible. Whilst he remained strangely resistant to horsemeat he was particularly keen for Britons to extend their dietary range as far as possible in order to avoid periodic shortages of more conventional fare.

Perhaps he had a point. After all, watching an African bushman eating maggots, a German eating pickled cabbage, a Bedouin munching on sheep's eyes or a Chinese tucking into a nice big bowl of steaming snake's head soup, it soon becomes clear that it is only culture which decides what is food and what is garbage. How else to explain why it is that, in England, we put salt on garden snails in order to kill them, whereas the French do it just to bring out the flavour?

But then again one man's meal is another man's poison, and anyone who thinks there are no fundamental differences between the nations is probably talking tripe as well as eating it. Certainly, that would explain why Mr Buckland and his Society for the Acclimatisation of Animals in the United Kingdom got it all so horribly wrong, and why most of the extraordinary dishes on the menu at the inaugural dinner on 12 July, 1862 were rarely, if ever, seen again.

After attending a Horseflesh Dinner at London's Langham Hotel – and trying horse soup, tongue, sausage, and various joints boiled and roast –

Buckland observed that 'hippophagy has not the slightest chance of success in this country'. But at his own event at Willis's Rooms, London, formerly the premises of Almack's in King Street, St James's, he offered a hundred diners a choice of several tried and tested Buckland family favourites including soups made from birds' nests, an elephant's trunk, porpoise-head slices (boiled and sliced) and rhino pie. There were also panther chops from London zoo, ants and earwigs, Japanese sea-slug or sea-cucumber and slug soup, kangaroo, parrot, wild boar and curassow – the latter a large Central American bird which is said to taste quite like pheasant.

The event was by all accounts successful, although a big thumbs-down went to sea-slug which (despite Buckland's optimistic description of it as 'succulent and pleasant and not unlike the green fat of a turtle') was described by one guest as a cross between calf's-head jelly and glue.

At one level, the founder of the Society was evidently a serious man who knew what he was about. A senior officer of the Piscatorial Society and professionally trained in surgery, Buckland subsequently became HM Inspector of Salmon Fisheries. He is also the author of the four-volume *Curiosities of Natural History*, although this last item contains a number of more left-field suggestions, such as exhorting readers to make inkstands from horse's hooves and spill-holders out of dried horse's ears.

Buckland had a keen, if wholly unscientific, interest in circus freaks and sideshow novelties too, and numbered among his friends the 'Great Zazel', a female who made a living being shot from a cannon, and a variety of dwarfs, giants and other physically odd human specimens. He was also known to frequent the premises of rat-catchers and taxidermists and was keen to understand if not acquire, their unique trade skills.

At home, he would eat mice on toast or dipped in batter and one of Buckland's in-laws recalled once tripping over a dead baby hippo which had been left at the foot of the stairs. Buckland's other pets included a variety of mongoose, an eagle, several red slugs, rats, a red river hog, a jackal and a bear named Tiglath-Pileser after a 3,000 year-old Assyrian king. The bear was something of a celebrity around Christ Church when Buckland was at Oxford and was introduced to a nephew of Napoleon's. On another occasion, it fell asleep in front of Florence Nightingale after being hypnotised.

As far as is known, Francis Buckland never recommended the consumption of family pets, however, and he died somewhat conventionally of dropsy or œdema whilst still in his fifties.

DR WILLIAM BUCKLAND
(1784–1856)

Like son like father

A leading 'undergroundologist' – his word –' of his day, William Buckland was Oxford's first professor of geology and while serving as Canon of Christ Church somehow found time to promote efficient drainage in London, to lobby for the use of gas to light the streets of Oxford, and for the employment of guano droppings as a plentiful source of fertiliser.

Today, however, he is mostly remembered for eating things – in particular the 100 year-old heart of a French king – and for a unique skill which enabled him to determine precisely where in the country he was simply by scooping up the top soil and placing it on his tongue.

Buckland was in short a man of rare tastes, honing his skills in this department by encouraging his family and their guests to eat everything from hedgehog to crocodile, roast bear to stuffed mice, a variety of insects and a cooked-up puppy. How that last went down is not recorded, but the hedgehog was generally favourably reviewed, although the crocodile was in the words of one otherwise satisfied house guest 'an utter failure'.

Buckland himself thought the most disgusting thing he'd ever eaten was a mole, but then he tried a bluebottle which was, by his own account, infinitely more repulsive. He also tried quite a few similarly stomach-churning alternatives, including the bones of St Rosalia of Palermo, afterwards telling an outraged Sicilian priest that in his view they were the bones of a goat, and a drop of the blood of a holy martyr. This he also dismissed, insisting it was in reality just bat urine, suggesting of course that he was already familiar with that particular flavour . . .

Buckland's most outstanding feat of zoophagy came later, however, when he visited his old friend, Edward Harcourt, Archbishop of York, and was shown a casket or snuffbox said to contain the shrivelled, embalmed heart of Louis XIV. (Harcourt had been in Paris during the Revolution, when presumably the organ in question had been 'liberated' by someone keen to take advantage of the chaos and anti-royalist feeling.) Observing that he had eaten many things 'but never the heart of a king', Buckland plucked it out and gobbled it down so that the precious if grisly relic is now gone for good.

JOHN MYTTON (1796-1834)

Filbert-powered sporting hero

With John Mytton it was more the booze than the food, and when prevailed upon to go to Cambridge after being sacked from both Westminster and Harrow – and even then agreeing to go only on the understanding that when he got there he would not be expected to open a single book, let alone read one – his first move was to order an astonishing 2,000 cases of port to be sent to his new college to await his arrival.

In the end, Mytton left them untouched, however, preferring to go on a Grand Tour of the Continent before securing a commission in the fashionable 7th Hussars and settling down to a lively year in and around London drinking and gambling and doing what young men do. He soon quit the regiment and, after coming into a very substantial fortune, made his exit by jumping his one-eyed charger Baronet over the mess table and heading for Shropshire.

Mytton's mind turned briefly to politics, and by the simple expedient of pinning £10 notes to his coat and encouraging the voting public to help themselves as he walked around town, he secured the seat of Shrewsbury. The tactic is thought to have cost him £10,000 (at a time when a bespoke gentleman's suit would have cost less than a tenner) although his interest in the workings of Parliament was such that when he entered the chamber for the first time he remained there only just long enough to be sworn in before leaving the building never to return.

Thereafter, Mytton concentrated mostly on drinking and sporting bets. A favourite morsel was a side-order of filberts (a close relation to the hazelnut) which he consumed in increasing vast quantities. In the absence of port – of which he was reckoned to have drunk six to eight bottles a day – he'd fasten upon anything else with a similar kick, including, it was said, eau-de-cologne if nothing else was on offer. He was also something of a shopaholic and, at one point, owned 150 pairs of riding breeches, 700 pairs of riding boots, around a thousand hats and three times that number of made-to-measure shirts.

Despite his daily intake, he was up for any challenge which called for physical exertion (the aforementioned horse, Baronet taking part in many of them, and faring better than another of Mytton's favourite mounts, Sportsman, which dropped dead after he fed it a pint of port to warm it up). Otherwise, for a wager, Mytton was known to wrestle bears, bite dogs,

chase rats across frozen lakes and hunt ducks naked. He even once attempted – and failed – to jump a tollgate with his carriage but more because it sounded exciting than to save a few pennies.

Less appealing, perhaps, was his violently laying into a Welshman who had attempted to head off his hounds (as well as squire, Mytton was the local Master). Having literally beaten him into submission, Mytton at least offered the poor man half a sovereign in recognition of a hard battle well fought.

Clearly he couldn't go on like this for ever, and in the end it all came to a pretty sudden halt. Just 15 years after coming into his giant inheritance he had spent the lot, lost his seat in Parliament and his ancestral home, and ended up in a debtor's cell. Bust, just 38, and in truly terrible shape, Mytton set light to his night-shirt one evening in an attempt to cure an attack of hiccoughs. Surprisingly, this radical and somewhat unorthodox antidote had the desired affect, but only because 'Mad Jack' Mytton was now as dead as a duck.

HELENA, COMTESSE DE NOAILLES
(1824–1908)

Dietary guru ahead of her time

Madame – as she liked to be called – was as English as they come, the daughter of a Baring and a niece to Lords Cromer and Revelstoke. However, after a brief marriage to a French count, she affected a certain Frenchness together with a strange dietary and health regime which never left her. Unfortunately, she also inflicted this on a Spanish girl whom she had purchased and adopted when the poor child was just nine years old.

Maria Pasqua was apparently bought for two bags of gold (or a vineyard, depending on who is telling the story) and sent to an English convent boarding school. With her went a list of requirements long enough to make the average modern molly-coddling parent look like they really couldn't care less what happened to their children once they'd packed them off to school.

For starters, the nuns were required to drain the school pond because Madame had a dread of flying insects (at home she kept a string of onions hanging by her bedroom door, presumably as some kind of odoriferous bug deterrent). Maria was also forbidden to do any work after 6pm, to receive any innoculations against any kind of illness, and in the event of her succumbing to bronchitis she was to be fed nothing but fresh herring roe.

The school also had to provide the little girl with her own cow so she would have ready access to clean, fresh milk just like her mother, and also a supply of methane which Madame obtained by tying up her own flatulent beast beneath her bedroom window. Very keen on the health-giving properties of milk, mutton and methane was Madame. Indeed, had the Comtesse been active a hundred years later she'd doubtless have been a natural for a string of dietary bestsellers on the 'M-Plan Diet' line and been given a regular slot on breakfast television.

Naturally, Maria wasn't to wear the standard school uniform either, but instead be dressed, or rather draped, in a Grecian tunic and a pair of hand-made leather sandals in order that as much fresh air as possible would be able to circulate freely about her person.

Unfortunately, these strictures continued well into Maria's adulthood so that when she married and became pregnant, she was still being repeatedly instructed to drink only water which had been boiled up with pine-needles. Also to ensure that every tree in the vicinity of her house had been culled in order to prevent her picking up something unpleasant from the bark. Madame also recommended that Maria never, ever travel when the wind was coming from the east, although the reason for this was not made entirely clear.

Despite her bossiness in such matters, it was frequently suspected that the Comtesse herself never actually ate the mutton she recommended so forcefully. This was because a screen was always placed around her at mealtimes lending support to the theory that whilst her guests struggled through their greasy stew, Madame was busy dipping into something far more toothsome.

The milk thing was certainly for real though, and she stuck with that until the end of her days. Family picnics, for example, would always be accompanied by a cow or two which would be milked directly into glasses before these were topped up with Cognac. In fact, later in life she lived almost entirely on milk and Champagne, a perfectly disgusting-sounding combination although she must have got something right because she lived until 84.

The Comtesse left a fortune when she died but also – alas – a dozen different wills, each containing different plans for the disposal of an estimated £100,000. Fortunately, all of these agreed that Maria should get the bulk of it – but only on condition that she dressed in white every day throughout the summer and never, ever laced-up her shoes.

MATTHEW ROBINSON, LORD ROKEBY
(1712–1800)

Of beef tea and beards

Where it was milk for Madame, the second Lord Rokeby would consume beef tea and little else. (He thought wheat was particularly exotic and entirely unsuitable for human consumption.) At least where the Comtesse sought to impose her will on her adopted daughter Maria, his Lordship's respect for democracy meant that he was happy for his guests to eat and drink whatever they chose.

The same respect also led Rokeby to resign as an MP soon after being elected, so shocked was he by the corruptness endemic in conventional party politics. Instead, he attempted to install his own brand of natural justice on his estate in Kent by refusing ever to raise the tenants' rent.

Rokeby also insisted that the fields of Mount Morris were to be farmed entirely according to his own radical views on agriculture and animal husbandry. For a start, this meant no fences and no closed gates, no trees ever to be felled on the 800 acres, and nothing to be planted or cultivated unless it grew naturally. Because of this, even his gardens were gradually returned to nature – or ruin, depending on your perspective – while his flocks and herds were allowed to roam and graze freely on the understandable grounds that cows and sheep probably knew better than man what was good for them and what was not.

Lord Rokeby took a similar approach to his personal grooming and at one time allowed his beard to run down to his knees and his moustaches – of which there were definitely two – to grow so long that he could flip one over each of his ears. He would walk everywhere too, being a big fan of fresh air and frequent exercise, although once again his sense of fairness meant that he was more than happy to have his servants follow on behind him in a carriage.

His other great health tip concerned the use of water, which he recommended to everyone for both internal and external applications. He set up drinking fountains all over his estate and provided small monetary rewards for any tenants or staff he observed drinking from them. Finally, he spent

many hours of each day immersed in the stuff, (going so far as to have a special bath house built with a thatched roof) beneath which he would sit up to his neck for hour after hour whilst he took meals, entertained visitors, and wrote a sequence of strange pamphlets setting out his various theories and political hopes. On at least one occasion, he was accompanied in this by a roast loin of veal which bobbed up and down beside him as he went through his daily routine.

As is usually the case, such firm preferences were accompanied by equally strong dislikes. Amongst those things Lord Rokeby really couldn't abide were doctors – his cure for everything seemed to be to open the windows and be sure to never light a fire – and the Governor and officers of the Bank of England. Such an institution, he insisted, was sure to fail in the end and indeed he was so sure of this that he not only made a substantial £10 bet on it with a Canterbury bigwig but took steps to ensure that his heirs would continue the bet in the event of his own death preceding the Bank's. The wager, presumably, is still running.

ECCENTRIC VENUES FOR DINNER

- Despite being consigned to the hellhole of Fleet Prison in 1596 for various financial irregularities Richard Stoneley, an official of the Exchequer, regularly entertained his wife and family in his cell where they enjoyed a calf's head, roast veal, boiled beef, and small gamebirds. Followed by cheese and fruit, their splendid dinner would be accompanied by plenty of claret and 'canary sack' or dry white wine.
- In 1905, American millionaire George A. Kessler entertained two dozen guests with a giant, flower-laden gondola floating in the flooded courtyard of London's Savoy Hotel. The courtyard was painted to resemble Venice, a giant birthday cake arrived on the back of an elephant and Caruso sang 'Happy Birthday.' The occasion was marred only by a quantity of dead swans which had been killed off by a toxic blue dye introduced into the hotel's temporary lagoon.
- In October 1843, 14 men sat down to a draughty dinner at the very top of what is still the world's tallest Corinthian column to celebrate the long overdue erection of a monu-

ment to Nelson. (Britain's naval hero had been dead for more than half a century by the time Landseer's lions were finally moved into place). Nelson himself was not present; his likeness being winched up only once the table and chairs had been cleared away.

- Marc Brunel organised an underwater banquet in September, 1827 in a bid to show that his new Thames Tunnel at Wapping was perfectly safe. The band of the Coldstream Guards was on hand to entertain 130 miners and 40 distinguished guests but, unfortunately, the tunnel which had already claimed the lives of several workers collapsed again soon afterwards and, the following January, the waters of the Thames rushed back in once more.
- On New Year's Eve, 1853, a dinner was held inside a partially completed iguanodon at Crystal Palace's celebrated Dinosaur Park. It was hosted by Professor of Anatomy, Richard Owen, based at the British Museum of National History and the man who first coined the term dinosaur meaning 'terrible lizard'. The toast on the evening was as follows:

  > *Saurians and Pterodactyls all!*
  > *Dream ye ever, in your ancient festivities,*
  > *Of a race to come, dwelling above your*
  >   *tombs,*
  > *Dining on your ghosts!*

- As work continues to convert Battersea's famous Grade II-listed power station into a 38 acre 'living, leisure and lifestyle space', developers have unveiled plans which include a private dining room at the top of one of the popular icon's four towering 350 ft chimneys.
- Perched on top of the Wellington Arch at Constitution Hill, Adrian Jones's gigantic winged figure of Peace standing in a chariot and pulling on the reins of four highly spirited stallions was the scene of a memorable dinner in 1912. The sculptor, a former officer in the Hussars, entertained seven guests to celebrate the conclusion of four years' work on his striking £17,000 bronze.

- Although the great cathedral of St Paul's will always be Sir Christopher Wren's, a new cross and ball were installed by the Surveyor to the Fabric, C.R. Cockerell, in 1820 to replace the weather-beaten originals. Once this had been done, a small celebratory lunch was held inside the golden ball.
- Despite licensing hours introduced at street level to keep munitions workers from drinking heavily during the Great War, there were more than 30 underground bars on the tube network including buffets at Sloane Square and Liverpool Street. The last, Pat Mac's Drinking Den on the Metropolitan Line, didn't close until 1978.

JOSHUA ABRAHAM NORTON
(1819–1880)

Ruined by rice

Joshua Norton – or as he preferred to be addressed, His Imperial Majesty Norton I, Emperor of the United States of America and Protector of

Mexico – was a Londoner whose family emigrated to South Africa before he himself moved on to California, managing along the way to build up an immense fortune by buying and selling various staples.

That Norton was bright there was no doubt, but he was also barmy enough to think he could corner the world market in rice and, in 1853, he set out to buy all of it that he possibly could. In this he was helped by a famine-struck China's refusal to allow any exports which quickly led the price in America to rocket from just four cents a pound to nearly 40. Unfortunately, he was hindered by the sheer volume of the stuff – even now, rice accounts for 20% of total human calorific intake – so that, once he had sunk his not inconsiderable fortune into buying many hundreds of tons of it, it took just one shipment from Peru to send the price back down again from where it had started.

Norton was suddenly broke, repeatedly in and out of court for non-payment of his trading debts, and his already shaky mental state soon suffered a serious fracture. By 1859, he was writing to the *San Francisco Bulletin* to declare himself the Emperor of the United States. (Prior to this, he had already alerted close friends to his secret status as Emperor of California but, upon discovering that the State lacked the legal where-withall to legitimise his position, he had clearly now decided to up the ante).

Norton's declaration spelt out the situation quite clearly: 'At the peremptory request and desire of a large majority of the citizens of these United States, I, Joshua Norton, formerly of Algoa Bay, Cape of Good Hope, and now for the last 9 years and 10 months past of S. F., Cal., declare and proclaim myself Emperor of these U. S.; and in virtue of the authority thereby in me vested, do hereby order and direct the representatives of the different States of the Union to assemble in the Musical Hall, of this city, on the 1st day of Feb. next, then and there to make such alterations in the existing laws of the Union as may ameliorate the evils under which the country is laboring, and thereby cause confidence to exist, both at home and abroad, in our stability and integrity.'

Somewhat surprisingly the Americans seem to have accepted it with good grace allowing Norton I to 'reign over' them for the next 21 years.

As part of his master plan, less than a month later, Norton abolished the Republic and the office of President, dissolved the US Congress, declared both the Republican and Democratic Parties to be null and void, and announced that from now on, he would rule personally. Furthermore, anyone treating his adopted home city with anything less than full respect – for example, by referring to it as 'Frisco' – would be deemed guilty of what His Imperial Majesty termed a High Misdemeanor and fined $25.

Inevitably, the odd attempt was made to silence him. In 1867, he was arrested on a charge of insanity but the public rose up in his defence and his accusers soon withdrew. For the remainder of his life, Norton enjoyed something akin to celebrity status, and would frequently appear in public dressed in a special blue and gold dress uniform and a beaver hat with a peacock feather which had been presented to him by a group of US Army officers. On these walkabouts, he would take time to inspect bus timetables and other aspects of city life, assuring his subjects that their wellbeing was his prime concern.

In return for this diligence on their behalf, his supporters took it upon themselves to pay for the upkeep of his Imperial Palace – actually a 50 cent-a-night bed in a rundown rooming house – whilst Norton was routinely fed and watered free of charge in the city's finest restaurants. The owners of many of these would thereafter attach brass plaques to their frontages declaring the premises to be 'By Appointment to His Imperial Majesty Emperor Norton of the United States.'

It was perhaps not surprising that rumours freely circulated suggesting that Norton was the son of Louis Napoleon. There was also the equally strongly held conviction amongst many San Franciscans that their man was in line to marry the widowed Queen Victoria. In any event, when his end came, he was afforded every possible courtesy. The *San Francisco Chronicle* ran the headline, 'Le Roi est Mort,', the *Morning Call* reserved its front page for the sad news that 'Norton the First, by the grace of God Emperor of these United States and Protector of Mexico, departed this life' and, across the Atlantic, Robert Louis Stevenson saluted him as a charming harmless madman.

A search of the 'Palace' revealed, unsurprisingly, that Norton had died a very poor man indeed. His possessions were limited to a solitary sovereign, an obsolete French franc, a collection of walking sticks, a bent sabre, several battered hats –including a stovepipe, a Derby, and a red-laced Army cap – and a handful of so-called Imperial Bonds which His Majesty was in the habit of selling to tourists with a fictitious return of 7%.

Clearly Norton was heading for a pauper's grave, but San Francisco smiled on him one more time and a number of benefactors stumped up for a rosewood casket before, by some accounts, as many as 30,000 of his subjects lined up along the streets and his cortege made its final journey. It was a fitting end for an emperor, especially one who, unusually for one in his position (and as the court records noted following his 1867 arrest), had 'shed no blood, robbed no one and despoiled no country'.

FRANCIS HENRY EGERTON, EARL OF BRIDGEWATER (1756-1829)

Dining with dogs

Contemptuous of his family, but clearly in thrall to its history and status, the 8th Earl of Bridgewater fell out badly with the 7th Earl (his brother) and expressed himself grossly disappointed in the Duke (his uncle) but when he came into the lesser title himself – and some £40,000 a year – this former vicar lost no time in applying the family arms to literally everything that he possibly could.

Generally Bridgewater preferred pets to people, in particular his cats and dogs, each of which was furnished with a silver collar bearing the family crest. His favourites were a pair of dogs named Bijou and Biche and he lived in Paris despite inheriting an elaborately Gothic ancestral home at Ashridge in Hertfordshire. Never much one for Parisian society – he spoke Latin more often than French – Bridgewater soon made a habit of taking his meals with them rather than with the very few of his own species with whom he might have fancied spending time.

Insisting the animals were well turned out – to which end he had boots and gowns made for them by the best makers of the day – Lord Bridgewater also required them to display the best possible manners once his footmen had tied linen napkins around their necks and put their mono-grammed plates before them. Those that didn't were consigned to the servants' hall for a week; a harsh sentence he clearly felt to be more than most well brought-up dogs would be able to bear.

On the rare occasions when a human was invited to join them they were guaranteed to be offered nothing more inviting than plain boiled beef, even though his modest city garden was crammed to the walls with 300 rabbits, 300 pigeons and 300 partridges at which he would occasionally take potshots whenever the yearning for a little sport overcame him.

His dogs accompanied him on his rides around Paris too, and the Bridgewater coach became a familiar sight around the streets of the city where it was instantly recognisable – not just by the crest on the doors, but by the silk cushions provided for the comfort of up to half a dozen canines at a time. Umbrella-wielding footmen were also on hand lest it rain when the entourage reached the Bois du Boulogne.

Whilst reportedly something of a slob when it came to his own table-manners, the dogs' master was, nevertheless, always immaculately dressed and famously never wore an item more than once. He also required his valet to keep and catalogue all his cast-offs in the order in which he had worn them, which perhaps explains why when the crazy English milord went travelling he required 16 carriages for his personal effects, and 30 servants to ensure that his daily routine went according to plan.

Curiously, when Bridgewater died, none of his animals received so much as a mention in his will; instead, the servants were each issued with a suit of mourning clothes, a cocked hat and three pairs of stockings, and instructed to keep his household running for a further two months as if their master were still alive. He left his money to charity, including a mammoth £8,000 to the author or authors of the best work on 'the Goodness of God as manifested in the Creation' – presumably because by then he no longer had any contact with his family and no-one he could call a friend.

Chapter Eight

Men of War

LT. COL. ALFRED WINTLE
(1897–1966)

Up and at 'em

BORN in Russia, schooled in France and educated in Germany, Lt. Colonel Alfred Daniel Wintle nevertheless got down on his knees every night of his life 'and thanked God for making me an Englishman'.

Wintle was a career cavalryman in the 1st Royal Dragoons – where else? – and sincerely believed that time spent anywhere but on the back of a horse was time spent for no purpose. He carried an umbrella wherever he went and regardless of the forecast. As he put it, this was because, 'no gentleman ever leaves home without one' although this declaration was invariably followed by another of his favourite *bon mots* which ruled that neither would a true gentleman ever unfurl said item in public.

Like many a serving officer, Wintle noted the date in his diary when the Great War came to an end. He was, however, more than a little impatient for the next one to begin, and on the following page formally declared a 'private war on Germany' and set about railing against the War Office whose sole function (he believed) was to ready the nation and its people for the next big scrap.

Given this, it was perhaps inevitable that when a new war did break out he found himself entirely dissatisfied with the way the authorities planned to deal with their historic enemy. Accordingly, he decided to have a go at them in his own special fashion and, failing to commandeer an airplane to get him to the front in double-quick time, found himself in the Tower awaiting a Court Martial after pulling a revolver on an Air Ministry official and discharging it into the hapless individual's desk.

Wintle's enthusiasm was characteristically undimmed by this minor setback and he took his batman with him into captivity to ensure his personal comfort. He then set about inviting so many different eminent and influential guests to dine with him each evening that, when his case finally came to trial, the higher echelons were sufficiently embarrassed to quietly drop all charges and arrange for him to be sent abroad.

Before long, the monocled Wintle was imprisoned as a spy in occupied France, and was recaptured after a courageous but unsuccessful escape. At this point, he refused to let his standards drop and famously took his Vichy captors to task for their scruffy demeanour. Deciding to go on a hunger strike until they smartened up their act, he was soon to be heard loudly and repeatedly insisting that, to a man, they were a shambles and, as such, wholly unfit to hold an officer in the King's Army.

Nearly two decades later, on ITV's *This is Your Life*, the head of the garrison in question admitted to an audience of literally millions that he and some 280 of his men had eventually switched sides 'entirely because of the Colonel's dauntless example and his tirade of abuse and challenge'. Clearly, the force of Wintle's personality was something to be reckoned with, as indeed he was to demonstrate soon after whilst in hospital following a fall from his horse.

During his confinement, he discovered that someone from his own regiment was in an adjacent bed, the young boy-trumpeter apparently suffering from the usually fatal combination of diphtheria and mastoiditis. Standing over him, Wintle roared, 'What's all this nonsense about you dying, man? You know it's an offence for a Royal Dragoon to die in his bed. You will stop dying at once, get up immediately and get your bloody hair cut!' Remarkably, the young man, Cedric Mays, did just that, later admitting 'after that I was too terrified to die.'

Eventually, forced to leave his beloved regiment and to accept retirement, Wintle settled down in rural Kent to write whilst continuing his personal one-man battle to defend what he saw as proper English standards of behaviour.

Inevitably, this sometimes brought him into trouble with the law, and on one occasion, having purchased a first-class rail ticket and finding no seat free, he took the driver's place and refused to give it up until an extra carriage was found for him. Wintle also served six months in the 'Scrubs' for debagging a bent solicitor, although he was later able to clear his name in a landmark case which, typically, he fought all the way to the House of Lords whilst representing himself the whole way.

Lt. Col. Wintle was tricky, prickly, troublesome and undoubtedly highly chauvinistic, but it is nevertheless hard not to miss the likes of a man who, in his own words, spent a lifetime fighting clots and eventually died of one. Cedric Mays played the good man out at Wintle's funeral service at Canterbury Cathedral, in the absence of the band of the Royal Dragoons which was serving overseas.

SIR CLAUDE CHAMPION DE CRESPIGNY, BART. (1847-1935)

One of the old school

History sadly fails to relate whether Sir Claude knew Wintle but it seems likely that, being cut from the same piece of hairy green tweed, the two of them would have had plenty to say to each other had they met over a couple of club-measures. Joining the Royal Navy at 13 and transferring to the King's Royal Rifle Corps five years later, De Crespigny, like Wintle, just couldn't wait to get stuck in.

Also, just like Wintle, he had little time for office types, particularly any of those pencil-necked bureaucrats who seemed determined to come between him and his rock-solid conviction that 'where there is a daring deed to be done, and in any part of the world, an Englishman should leap to the front to accomplish it'.

De Crespigny felt that fighting was the only true indicator of character and a properly manly occupation. In peacetime he frequently offered a thrashing to anyone who he felt deserved it whilst expressing a sincere regret that duelling was no long legal. For a man of honour such as himself, his obituary in the *Times* noted, nothing else came close to a duel – guns, swords, knives or fists – when it came to sorting out a difference between two parties.

Clearly keen to extend the privilege of combat to the lower orders during an unwelcome lull in international hostilities, De Crespigny also decided to institute a new rule at his home, the aptly named Champion Lodge at Heybridge in Essex. From now on, he insisted, no man would be taken on to the staff before first going a few rounds with his would-be employer. Win or lose, he'd get the job providing he had showed sufficient spirit.

Tramps in the vicinity of the estate would similarly be offered the chance to box for a hot dinner and, to his credit, Sir Claude always kept up his end of the deal even when some muckers organised a 'ringer' by paying a professional pugilist to dress as a tramp and position himself by one of the gate lodges. Before long, Sir Claude duly appeared, threw down the expected challenge and promptly received the expected beating. Fortunately, he saw the funny side of this, and the boxer was invited back for supper.

Otherwise, in the absence of a good war to fight, he was always looking out for new trials of another sort and must have been particularly disappointed when, in 1869, Henry Morton Stanley turned down his offer to accompany him on his expedition to locate Dr Livingstone. (Stanley did so on the eminently sensible grounds that he, Sir Claude, had no actual experience of the dark continent. Not that this was De Crespigny's fault, you understand but, for a number of reasons, he had as he put it been unable 'to take part as a volunteer in several of our little African wars'.)

The tightrope-walker, Blondin, similarly refused him permission to have a go on the wire stretched tightly across Niagara Falls and, although De Crespigny succeeded in being posted to Egypt in 1889 to cover some Dervish-inspired unpleasantness or other for the *Sporting Times*, the authorities refused to accept that he was a genuine war correspondent –

or, indeed, that such a newspaper would even employ one. In the end, he never made it to the front or into the thick of the Boer War a few years later.

De Crespigny was a trier, though, you had to give him that and, as well as successful postings to India and Ireland (where he proved himself a first class steeple-chaser), he undertook a number of daredevil challenges clearly intended to give him the endorphin rush he so badly needed. In 1883, he and a colleague became the first men ever to fly a balloon across the North Sea. At the age of 42, despite having broken more than a dozen bones, he succeeded in swimming the Nile Rapids which no European had ever managed to do before. (Flushed with his success here, and naturally keen that his children should also be good swimmers, he taught them how to do it by pushing them off his boat and leaving them to work out how to swim to safety.)

After this, and for the rest of his life, De Crespigny was acknowledged as a sportsman of great ability, with even the *New York Times* identifying him as someone able to 'hunt like a hound, swim like a fish, run like a hare and box like [James J.] Jeffries'. Curiously, after his death, it also became apparent that Sir Claude had worked occasionally as an assistant hangman at Carlisle, on which occasions he employed the *nom de noose* of Charles Maldon – taking the name from his local town.

MAJOR BETTY HUNTER COWAN
(1912–1991)

Celebrated cavewoman

With echoes of John Betjeman's famous gel, Major Betty was a head girl of the old school who, after serving with distinction in the Women's Royal Army Corps in the 1940s, retired to Cyprus with her colleague-in-arms, Major Phylis Heymann.

The two remained on the island for the next 45 years and were known as 'the Cavewomen'. This was nothing to do with their appearance, simply that their hilltop address was Cave House, Tjiklos. They themselves preferred to be known as 'Wracks' and 'Cranks', however, after Major Betty's beloved WRAC and the Queen Alexandra's Royal Army Nursing Corps in which Major Phylis had served.

Unfortunately for the pair, during the EOKA troubles in the 1950s, and the civil war a decade later, it became apparent that Cave House (with its high elevation and uninterrupted view of the coast) was likely to come under attack. Repeatedly, the two women were urged to move on but, characteristically, they refused to do so and, instead, took responsibility for billeting and feeding scores of refugees as well as organising them into an effective fire-fighting force when the surrounding pine forests were in danger of burning to the ground.

Their courage and fortitude throughout this period was clearly considerable, but then their unflappable, matter-of-fact approach to these small local difficulties was perhaps no more than one would have expected from two true daughters of the Empire. This was perfectly illustrated on the occasion when a wounded Turkish soldier appeared in the garden and shot himself dead. Major Phylis, referring to the incident years later, admitted that they had felt rather sorry for him 'but I think he did the right thing.'

Betty and Phylis had rented Cave House from a local friend for £15 a month and continued to make friends on the island even when, to their initial dismay, the local Greek town became a Turkish one. Following the invasion, when most ex-pats went home or relocated to the island's southern half, the two decided to stay on although, throughout the 1970s, they insisted on making a weekly excursion to the Greek half of the island to see a film show organised by the British Council. A measure of their popularity can be gauged from the fact that the B.C. quickly agreed to make this a matinée performance in order that the Majors could make it back across the border before the Turks' 5pm curfew closed the frontier.

GEORGE HANGER, LORD COLERAINE
(1751–1824)

Goosed by turkeys

Although he had finished fighting by the time he was 22, George Hanger nevertheless found time to join up with the 1st Regiment of Footguards, the Hessian Jägers and, later, the British Legion's Light Dragoons, whilst picking up a wound in the American War of Independence. Reaching the rank of Colonel, and fighting at least three duels, he married a gipsy woman although she had run off with a tinker by the time he succeeded to his title.

After this, though later appointed Captain-Commissary in the Royal Artillery, Hanger settled down to have fun. Accordingly, he spent some time at court – he was a good friend of the Regent and, as a dandy, is reputed to have been the first man in England to wear a silk coat – but, to Hanger having fun mostly meant indulging in a series of increasingly daft wagers and, unfortunately, this, in turn, meant ending up broke.

Like so many Eighteenth Century blades, he would bet on anything – two raindrops running down a window, which of his fellow clubmen would die first, etc. – but his most celebrated bet was on a ten-mile race between a gaggle of geese and a flock of turkeys, a wager he eventually lost when the turkeys refused to play ball. The experience cost Hanger £500, equivalent to nearly twice the rent for a large house in Mayfair and, by 1798, he found himself in King's Bench Gaol after living way beyond his means for more than a decade.

As we've seen before, it was perfectly possible to live in these places in some comfort, providing one's friends came forward with money for food, bedding and even live-in servants. None of Hanger's friends did, however, and he languished there in considerable squalour for nearly a year and a half before his debts were paid off and he was allowed to leave.

Unsurprisingly, perhaps, Col. Hanger was a changed man. He threw off his old life and his smart friends, took on the job of a coal merchant and stuck at it for a full four years before the death of one brother (the 2nd

Baron) and then another (the 3rd) left him with a title. But this pleased him not at all, and for the rest of his life anyone who addressed him by it was ticked off with a curt, 'Plain George Hanger, if you please.'

The Prince Regent was none too happy at this and their friendship did not survive. Revelling in his newly democratic way of life, the 4th and last Lord Coleraine nevertheless decided to set out his stall in a volume which he called *The Life, Adventures, and Opinions of Col. George Hanger.* With the emphasis firmly placed on the third of these, most of his advice was directed at the ladies.

For example, the then-current fashion for large, loose gowns was applauded by Hanger as being appropriate to conceal both the bulk of a fat woman and the swag of anyone indulging in a little shoplifting. Girls considering elopement were similarly advised to leave by a window not the door, thereby establishing themselves in an heroic role and showing their men they were full of 'spirit, courage and spunk'. Beggar-women were also encouraged to find themselves blind men as companions, and Hanger took the opportunity to persuade village priests to effect the necessary introductions.

Finally, said Hanger, the government should bring in a new tax payable by any Scotsman who strayed over the border for more than six months at a time, although just where the inspiration came for that one is rather hard to say.

CLOTWORTHY SKEFFINGTON, EARL OF MASSERENE (1742–1805)

Prison volunteer with a difference

Only 16 when he inherited his father's title and fortune – and the family seat at Antrim castle – the 2nd Earl had the misfortune to find himself charged with some kind of business fraud whilst in France in 1770. He clearly had no idea what it was but, sooner than compensate the victims, he elected to spend a quarter of a century in gaol after which, under French law, the debt would be written off.

In the event, Masserene served a full 19 years and was released by the mob the very day before the storming of Bastille in 1789. Although he made a couple of half-hearted attempts to escape before this, the truth was that he'd probably not had a bad time of it. Dispensing an estimated £4,000 a year to ensure that his incarceration was made as comfortable as possible, he had received frequent visits from a whole string of mistresses, and his private chef came by daily to make sure his cuisine was up to snuff when he was entertaining guests.

During his time at the gaol at La Force, Lord Masserene also struck up a friendship with the Governor's daughter, whom he eventually married. Clearly it was a love-match (when Marie-Ann's favourite dog died, he dressed dozens more of them in white scarves and had them form up into a guard of honour) but, unfortunately, when she died at the turn of the century he remarried, too quickly and very unwisely. As a result, he lived to see wife number two, a former servant girl, siphoning off much of the Masserene fortune.

For now all that was in the future though and, free of gaol, the un-fortunately named Clotworthy set about surprising everyone by returning to Antrim Castle and forming his own private army. A fierce and vocif-erous opponent of the Jacobite cause, he was confident that he had everything he needed to take the fight to the enemy; enthusiasm, drive, men – everything, in fact, except guns and ammunition.

Undeterred by this tiny omission, Masserene set about establishing his

own yeomanry to defend the Castle and its hinterland, encouraging his troops to clap their hands in order to simulate rifle shots and later devising a complicated system of hand-gestures and semaphore in place of the conventional presentation of arms.

Encouraged by his apparent expertise in this new field of endeavour, he supplemented elements of the usual army exercises and drill with various new sequences designed wholly by himself. Unfortunately, particularly given their intriguing names – Eel-in-the-Mud was one, the Serpentine another – the precise choreography of his moves seems not to have been written down and is now lost forever. Sadly, it was also Masserene's fate to be largely ignored by the military establishment which, whilst it recognised his commitment and drive, remained wholly unconvinced by his unorthodox approach and so declined his offer to join his forces to their own.

ORDE WINGATE
(1903–1944)

Impressive but unorthodox

Tragically short-lived but a legitimate war-hero who more than matches the legend, Major Orde Charles Wingate DSO was as brilliant as he was bizarre, an efficient dynamo who rarely stayed still for long, and a masterful military technician who time and again during World War II proved the worth of 'thinking outside the box'.

Wingate's mother was a missionary with the Plymouth Brethren, and his father something of a martinet, so his upbringing in India was strict, to say the least, involving as it did an awful lot of forced marching.

His early education also bred in him an almost mystical regard for the teachings of the Old Testament, so that, having become something of a Zionist during the war, he seriously considered leading an attack against an Arab battalion using the traditional Jewish *shofar* or ram's horn until it became apparent that the Quartermaster could provide him only with the usual, standard-issue bugle.

More than 60 years after his death in an airplane crash over Burma, Wingate is these days (and quite rightly) remembered as the man behind

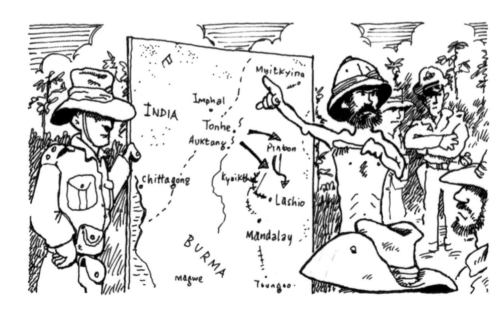

the Chindits – a highly effective long-range penetration unit employed fighting the Japanese behind the lines in Burma – and the so-called Gideon Force which combined British, Somali and Abyssinian troops to attack Mussolini's men in North Africa.

Here, in the field, he clearly knew what he was doing. Four Chindits won the VC and, although it numbered a mere 1,700 in total, Gideon Force on one occasion took the surrender of more than 20,000 Italians. But there was another side to Wingate, and one so odd that, without some very significant protectors – Churchill and General Wavell to name the two biggest – the chances are he would have swapped high command for a padded cell long before the war reached its happy conclusion.

For example, he maintained a fairly strange diet when he was in the tropics, often eating nothing but pounds of raw onions and grapes for days on end. He would wear at least one onion on a string round his neck to snack on and this was usually strung alongside a small alarm clock which, when it went off, was a signal to his interlocutors to stop talking now and leave him alone. Wingate also refused to wash for much of his life – from somewhere he had come to the conclusion that bathing was unhealthy – and instead he would use a rubber brush or an old toothbrush to scrub himself clean from top to toe.

Doing it that way naturally took time, which is perhaps one of the reasons why Wingate spent so long in the buff, frequently holding his regular strategy meetings in the nude (fortunately his officers and men were not expected to follow suit) while he scrubbed away. He even greeted eminent guests in this state and on more than one occasion.

As an Army officer, he of course had a uniform, but this he very deliberately kept in a disgraceful state as a way of expressing his somewhat iconoclastic disregard for conventional measures of rank. At other times, he appeared wearing nothing but a shower cap, so it is little wonder that the diaries of Lord Moran, Churchill's personal physician, record their meeting with the terse comment, 'Wingate hardly sane . . . in medical jargon a borderline case.'

ECCENTRIC LONDON PUBS

- The Mayflower (Rotherhithe Street, SE16) has for years held a unique licence to sell British and American postage stamps, thanks to its long ties with the former colony whose Pilgrim Fathers set off from the pub's back steps.

- Despite – or perhaps because of – its proximity to the House of Commons, the Silver Cross (Whitehall, SW1) is still licensed as a brothel because no-one has seen fit to revoke the licence granted by Charles I.
- The pub with the strangest name, however, is the I Am The Only Running Footman (Charles Street, W1). Formerly the Running Horse, it was renamed in the 1770s by the 4th Duke of Queensbury in honour of his own manservant who was said to be able to keep up a respectable 8 mph.
- The Lamb & Flag (Rose Street, WC2) was for years better known as The Bucket of Blood, so ferocious were the many prize-fights staged on the premises.
- Once a year at the Widow's Son (Devons Road, E3), a sailor hangs a hot-cross bun over the bar in a ritual stretching back more than two centuries. In so doing, he commemorates a real widow who, expecting her son home for Easter, kept a warm bun for him. Sadly, he never returned but each year until her death, she added another bun to the moulding, blackened bundle – the same bundle which is still preserved today.
- Ye Olde Cheshire Cheese (Fleet Street, EC4) is named after Sixteenth Century landlord, Thomas Cheshire, whom records show kept the tavern here in 1543. One of his successors had a parrot who achieved a measure of celebrity in 1918 by fainting after mimicking 400 bottles of Champagne popping open to mark the Armistice. Its vocabulary was so blue and so extensive that when it died, aged 40 in 1926, the BBC accorded it a unique honour and announced its demise on the wireless.
- At the Magpie & Stump (Old Bailey, EC4), it used to be more expensive to drink upstairs as it had a good view of the public hangings at the old Newgate Gaol opposite. The pub is still a favourite watering hole for lawyers and one room is traditionally known as Court No. 10; Nos. 1 to 9 being across the road in the Old Bailey.
- Finally, to the famous Bride of Denmark (Queen Anne's

Gate, SW1). This is London's only private public house and the brainchild of Hubert de Cronin, an architectural writer who rescued scores of fixtures and fittings from the many historic pubs destroyed in the Blitz. He installed the very best of these rescued fragments, including a majestic stuffed lion in a glass case, a wealth of engraved and cut glass, carved wood and fine panelling, in a warren of Victorian-style rooms beneath the offices of the Architectural Press. The Bride is now a private drinking club for staff members and their friends.

CHAPTER NINE

Finally, In Memoriam

⟫◆⟪

GENERAL JAMES M. BARRY
(c.1792-1865)

Dial M for Mystery

URIED at Kensal Green, which for years was London's most fashionable burial ground, General Barry keeps company with Blondin,
two children of George III, Thackery, Trollope and Sir Marc
Isambard Brunel. When the General died in 1865, he had good reason to
feel confident that history would show this one time senior Inspector of the
Army Medical Department to have been a fine soldier and an absolutely first
class medico-military administrator.

Unfortunately, fate intervened pretty rudely and, within hours of his
death, it was discovered that Barry was really a woman. The 'M' actually
stood for Miranda, and concealing the truth of this all her life, this quite
remarkable individual had nevertheless managed to rise to the very peak of
her profession. Indeed, only posthumously has the lady in question been
recognised as the first ever qualified female doctor – never mind the two
Elizabeths, Blackwell and Garrett Anderson – and the first lady general by
a century or more.

Amazingly, and despite her being described by several acquaintances as
'the most wayward of men' and in appearance 'beardless', not even the
General's closest associates had ever succeeded in guessing the truth.
Inevitably, there were plenty who later claimed always to have known it,
although it is significant that none came forward before the facts were
finally revealed.

In fact, only one witness ever actually wrote his suspicions down and, in
1817, the Count de Las Cases recorded in his book, *Journal of the Private
Life and Conversations of the Emperor Napoleon at St. Helena*, 'a visit from

one of the captains of our station. Knowing of the state of my son's health, he brought a medical gentleman with him . . . the Doctor, who was presented to me as a boy of 18, [had] the form, manners and voice of a woman. But Mr. Barry, such was his name, was described to be an absolute phenomenon. I was informed that he had obtained his diploma at the age of 13, after the most rigid examination, and that he had performed extraordinary cures at the Cape.'

Even so, the truth is that we are still not quite there yet, and not just because the military authorities kept their own records of the event secret for the next hundred years. Even now there's still a question mark over the General's earliest years, although there is a body of evidence which suggests her real name was Mary-Anne or Margaret Ann Bulkley, an Irish girl who adopted the name of her uncle when she decided to go under-cover.

It is not known whether the decision to do this was entirely her own, since it has also been suggested that the General's mother and uncle connived in the concealment in order to get the child into the medical school attached to the University of Edinburgh. Later, with the deception apparently complete, 'Miranda' signed on as a student at both Guys' and St Thomas' hospitals in London, before passing a series of exams set by the Royal College of Surgeons of England.

Bulkley/Barry joined the Army upon qualifying, and soon set sail for Cape Town, where she performed one of the first successful caesarian sections of modern times to deliver a healthy boy who was promptly named James Barry Munnik. Thereafter, her progress through the ranks was pretty spectacular and, although at one point demoted to Staff Surgeon after unwisely dallying in the hot-house politics on the island of St Helena, and temporarily struck down by yellow fever, Barry eventually assumed command over all military health establishments before reluctantly retiring in 1864 and dying of dysentery less than a year later.

SIR ROBERT MCALPINE (1847-1934)

On time and on budget

In a quiet corner of Surrey's Cobham Cemetery, an unusual mausoleum, dated 1934, houses the mortal remains of Sir Robert McAlpine, 1st Baronet. It is unusual mainly because it is of concrete rather than brick or good carved stone – but then that's perhaps only to be expected as its incumbent used the material to become Britain's greatest builder of the inter-war years. Not bad for someone who started his working life down a coalmine at the age of only ten.

Most famously, 'Concrete Bob', as he became known, built the original Wembley Stadium, completing it on time and on budget although the lessons on how to do this seem since to have been forgotten. His company was also responsible for Scotland's 21-arch Glenfinnan Viaduct which, when it was completed in 1901, was the largest concrete construction anywhere in the world.

Later, the same material was used to build the new Dorchester Hotel in Park Lane, a radical improvement on the original which had just a single bathroom for 40 bedrooms. Dried seaweed was used for sound insulation between each floor and, eventually, the Dorchester took Sir Robert into the hotel business on his own account: when the original client couldn't pay his bill, he kept the hotel. In the Blitz, Sir Robert's faith in concrete was further vindicated when, rumoured to be bombproof, his hotel became the air-raid shelter of choice for London's demi-monde.

Sadly though, whilst the company bearing his name still soldiers on, the McAlpine dynasty itself proved far less durable than the concrete on which its foundations depended. His son, another Sir Robert, succeeded him in the baronetcy but died just two weeks later and, whilst another son followed him into the construction business, things went sour here too when Sir Robert McAlpine sued Alfred McAlpine over use of the word 'McAlpine'. Mcbugger.

DR WILLIAM PRICE (1800–1893)

Burn baby burn

Dr Price was a man of strong opinions. For example, he felt marriage made slaves of women so his many children were all bastards. He was also a vegetarian nearly a century before it became fashionable, railed constantly against the perils of tobacco and vaccinations and, as the self-appointed Archdruid of All Wales, liked nothing more than to spend his free time gambolling naked in the hills above his Llantrisant home accompanied by a bevy of similarly nude female acolytes.

Clearly a bit much for most buttoned-up Victorians, Dr Price reserved his greatest enthusiasm for cremation. Finding nothing in this then highly controversial practice to counter his belief in reincarnation, he soon found himself in the dock charged with obstructing the course of an inquest after organising the burning of a body. At the same time, he was charged with attempting to dispose of a body by burning when the law required said body to be buried in suitably hallowed ground.

The body in question belonged to that of his young son – who, incidentally, he christened Jesus Christ – and as a keen and contentious litigant, Price clearly enjoyed the fight to clear his name. He also put on a bit of a show while he was at it, appearing in court in his Archdruid's get-up and conducting his defence in a strange combination of old Welsh and cabalistic linguistics. He felt cremation was more hygienic than burial but also, as an Archdruid, required his son to be reduced to ashes rather than interred under the ground

He won on the first count pretty quickly after producing a signed death certificate in court which proved that the boy had died of natural causes. And when it came to the second charge, he gleefully entered into battle by challenging the court to produce a single piece of legislation which rendered the burning of a human body an illegal act.

The court's response was to produce the testimony of a vicar but (as was only to be expected of the father of a child called Jesus Christ) Dr Price fulminated against the system and declared that the Church was not the same as the Law. Somewhat irritated by this controversial outburst, and dismissive of the doctor's claim that the gibberish he was spouting was the 'ancient tongue of the Welsh bards', presiding judge, Mr Justice Stephenson promptly had Price removed from the court to cool off after warning him that he faced a third charge of contempt if he didn't pipe down.

When he returned, Price had the good sense to remove his druidical gear, and sat quietly listening to the witness' testimony. Unfortunately, he also took the opportunity to berate the judge as a mere appointee of the relatively new and unproven Christian church, claiming that he, Price, had gained his own position by the grace of the god of the infinitely more ancient order of Welsh druidism.

Surprisingly, the judge took all this in relatively good humour, and the court settled down to hear testimony to the effect that, whilst he was undoubtedly a Grade One weirdo, Price was by most accounts a good doctor who, professionally at least, was held in high esteem by the local population. Equally surprisingly the jury eventually proved unable to reach a verdict, so a retrial was ordered only to be cancelled immediately when it became apparent that the police no longer wished to press charges.

Judge Stephenson was clearly relieved at this, but Price was furious and – never one to accept a gift horse for what it was – immediately launched his own suit against the police, accusing them of malicious prosecution, wrongful imprisonment and defamation of character. This new case came to court six months later. A new jury found for Dr Price, but set damages at just one farthing which presumably says something about their own thoughts on his character.

Price felt the outcome was nevertheless a good one, with cremation now established as an acceptable, legal practice and one suitable for everyone, not just druids. Even so, contentious litigant that he was – for which read awkward bugger – when his own time came, at the age of 93, Price hit the headlines once again. It emerged from his will that far, from consigning his own body to one of the new, official crematoria 'specially constructed with regenerative and reverberating furnaces according to the Italian model', he fancied a public burning and wanted his corpse dressed and seated on an ancient throne placed atop two tons of coal on the summit of Caerlan Hill.

The authorities were naturally horrified but, eventually, in the spirit of compromise, it was agreed that, providing the body was 'decently shrouded' in a coffin, the performance – for that's what it was – could go ahead. It duly did, and, watched by some 20,000 spectators, Dr Price finally ascended in his preferred manner to the heavens – or wherever it is that Archdruids go to await their eventual reincarnation.

SIR RICHARD BURTON (1821–1890)

The Original Tricky Dicky

Not to be confused with the much-married Welsh actor of the same name, who was, anyway, christened Jenkins, Captain Sir Richard Burton KCMG FRGS was an aggressive self-publicist as well as a renowned explorer. He was also a writer and poet with more than 40 volumes to his credit, a soldier, diplomatist, orientalist, ethnologist, linguist, hypnotist and an expert fencer when he wasn't busy translating the *Arabian Nights*.

In particular, he was keen to advertise his own exploits, to which end he asked his long-suffering wife to ensure that, when the time came, his

mortal remains be interred in an Arab 'tent', thereby providing a neat reminder for future generations that here was a Great Man, the first infidel ever to penetrate the secret Mohammedan citadel of Mecca.

A committed Christian, Lady Burton didn't entirely approve of all this. Nor, for that matter, of her husband's world-class collection of porn-ography which he had amassed over many years from every corner of the globe. Or, indeed, of his diaries which she famously burned after his death thereby earning the undying fury of generations of biographers as yet unborn.

Lady Burton, nevertheless, did as she was asked, although she took the opportunity to mix conventional Christian iconography with his preferred Islamic decoration of crescents and stars. Quite against his wishes, she also ensured that he – and later she, when she joined him – were laid to rest in consecrated ground.

In fact, she had originally attempted to secure her husband a place in Westminster Abbey, preferably alongside Livingstone whose equal she felt him to be. Not surprisingly, the Abbey authorities bridled at this, finding abhorrent many of Burton's libertarian views, aspects of his lifestyle and his professed conversion to Islam. Because of this, Lady Burton had to make do with this small Catholic burial ground at Mortlake in south-west London.

A century later, the mausoleum with its little crucifix on top still looks pretty eccentric, but then Burton was never one to blend in and one suspects that, even with his wife's alterations, he'd probably approve. Though somewhat out of sorts in the suburbs with its Islamic decoration, it is still definitely worth a visit – the gloomy interior can be glimpsed through a small window at the back – assuming you can find it.

MEMENTO MORI – ECCENTRIC EPITAPHS

- At the army church of St Mary Magdalene at Woolwich in south-east London, a plaque records the following: 'Sacred to the Memory of Major James Brush who was killed by the accidental discharge of a pistol by his orderly 14th April 1831. Well done, o good and faithful servant'.
- But then, if memorable memorials to the dead are what you seek, London's churches and churchyards have more than a few to make you smile. The burial register at Shoreditch in the East End, for example, records the death of Thomas Cam, easily London's oldest old-boy at the age of 207.
- Tom lacks a stone, but one within the precincts of Westminster Abbey commemorates a relative junior named 'Old Parr' who perished at just 152 years young. By a happy quirk of fate, the Abbey also acknowledges longevity in the animal kingdom and the oldest stuffed bird in England (a parrot, since you ask) can be found with the effigy of Frances Stuart, wife of the late Duke of Richmond and Lennox. She found fame, incidentally, posing as Britannia for the coins minted during the reign of Charles II.
- Today, it seems unlikely the Abbey authorities would allow even a Duchess such a singular display, still less the rest of us. Instead, modern churchyard administrators with their statutes, rules and regulations prefer discretion and simplicity every time. The sort of thing exemplified by two headstones found east of the City. One, at St Michael's, Crooked Lane, states simply: 'Here lyeth wrapped in clay/The body of William Wray/I have no more to say'. And the other, back at Shoreditch, is even better: 'Exit Burbage, 1619'.

FRANCIS JACK NEEDHAM, EARL OF KILMOREY (1787–1880)

A final, final resting place

Buildings occasionally move location. For instance, London's Temple Bar was shipped out of the City to Hertfordshire and then back again, whilst the old London Bridge is, these days, to be seen in Arizona's Lake Havasu City. But you could be forgiven for thinking a mausoleum would stay put, or at least not make a habit of moving every time its owner fancied a change of scene. Well you could, but you'd be mistaken, at least when it comes to the highly decorated Egyptian mausoleum built by Francis Jack Needham, 2nd Earl of Kilmorey, for his mistress.

Kilmorey inherited considerable wealth and a title from a hero of the Irish Rebellion – the actions of his father, 12th Viscount and 1st Earl, had proved decisive in the 1798 Battle of Arklow – and built the mausoleum for his mistress, Priscilla Anne Hoste, on whom he had fathered a son before she died at their house in London in 1854.

The mausoleum was designed by Henry Kendall Snr. and erected at Brompton Cemetery at a cost said to be close to £30,000, at a time when a match girl could reasonably expect to make less than ten shillings a week.

The style of the Nile was clearly very much in vogue in the 1850s, and Kendall was apparently one of its masters having published several similarly themed designs for the inhabitants of the aforementioned and highly fashionable Kensal Green Cemetery. He built a neat funerary temple of pink and grey granite for Kilmorey's mistress, before turning his attention to the alteration of his Lordship's latest acquisition, Twickenham's historic Orleans House.

The nobleman, it transpired, was also something of a nomad. In Ireland, he called his 55,000 acre estate at Mourne Park home but he liked to keep on the move while in England and is recorded as buying, remodelling and selling several significant houses in this area. Little surprise then that, before long, he had lost interest in Orleans House (formerly the home of Louis Philippe, Duc d'Orléans and, from 1830 to 1848, France's 'Citizen King') and moved to Woburn Park in Weybridge, Surrey, taking the mausoleum with him so it could be rebuilt close by.

That was in 1862, but, within six years, Kilmorey was off again, this time back to Twickenham and Gordon House which, whether he remembered or not, he had previously owned back in the early 1850s. Once more, the mausoleum was dismantled, moved and re-erected, but this time for the last time – one imagines – since the Earl rejoined his beloved upon his own death in 1880.

Kilmorey it seems was a bit of a tunneller too, having burrowed beneath the present-day Kilmorey Road in order that, when the time came, he could be conveyed across to his mausoleum without being seen. One suspects he would not be sorry when he got there. Not just because the Needhams' family motto was the eminently sensible *Nunc aut numquam* (now or never), and not just because he would now be even closer to his beloved Priscilla. But also because, as his biographer has noted, aside from loathing socks and moving house more than was good for him, the Earl's other personal eccentricities included kipping in his coffin and having his man wheel him back and forth to the mausoleum whilst he reclined in the box, trying it out for size.

Now it was his for good. The Earl was then rumoured to have been buried in it wearing a dressing gown fashioned from rats' fur.

HANNAH BESWICK (1680–1758)

Better safe than sorry

Director and comedy actor Woody Allen once denied being scared of dying – admitting only that he didn't want to be there when it happened – but Hannah Beswick's relationship with the Grim Reaper sounds a little bit more complex.

It wasn't that she was scared, exactly, just that when the time came for her to leave Cheetwood Hall, Manchester, she really didn't want to risk being buried alive. Besides being something of a fashionable fear at the time, this had been given added piquancy a few years before when one of Miss Beswick's brothers awoke from a deep trance just as the final nails were being driven into his coffin . . .

To avoid the same thing happening to her, Hannah arranged things so that, when the time came for her to make her own final journey (in 1758 when she was 78), her doctor was detailed to receive some £25,000 in her will on condition that he visited her regularly. He was also required to examine her to see whether or not she was OK, and to determine whether there was any chance that she might be revived.

A professional to his fingertips, the doctor took his charge seriously (mind you, £25,000 was quite a serious inducement in the mid-Eighteenth Century) and, after having Miss Beswick carefully embalmed with tar and bandages, he installed her in a glass-fronted grandfather clock. He kept this at the top of his stairs to avoid shocking any unsuspecting visitors, to which end he covered the clock with a heavy velvet curtain. Thereafter, once a year and for the next 55 years, the doctor walked upstairs, drew back said curtain and, in front of witnesses, satisfied himself – and them – that Hannah Beswick, now 133 years old, was still definitely dead.

The story does not quite end there. Because Hannah's will required her body to be kept above ground for a full 100 years, the grisly relic eventually had to be removed from the doctor's house to the local Lying-in Hospital. Then, when the hospital closed, it was moved on again to the Manchester Museum of Natural History. According to contemporary reports, it quickly became 'an object of much popular interest' amongst visitors to the museum.

The body remained there until 1868 when Hannah Beswick was finally and officially declared dead at the age of 188. In July of that year, her body was moved for the fourth, and it is to be hoped final time, to an unmarked plot in Manchester's General Cemetery where after a proper Christian burial the 'Manchester Mummy' was committed to the ground at last.

ADELINE, 'COUNTESS OF LANCASTER' (1825–1915)

Dressed to offend

When she wasn't busy rehearsing her death and lying-in, state, the Countess of Cardigan, also known as Comtesse de Lancastre, and Countess of Lancaster (she mischievously encouraged the anglicisation of her name) the former Miss Adeline Louisa Maria de Horsey displayed an almost teenage determination to offend others by behaving badly.

Of course in Victorian society that wasn't so hard to do and today one is inclined to smile at the idea that anyone might be seriously outraged at Adeline smoking cigarettes in public or daring to go out on a bicycle dressed in her husband's old regimental trousers. But Adeline knew exactly what she was up to, and would have known all too well that, far from being hers, the title 'Countess of Lancaster' was instead one of Queen Victoria's preferred aliases when she wished to travel around her realm *incognito*.

Picking a fight with one's monarch was, of course, far from clever, but in Adeline's opinion, Queen Victoria had started it by refusing ever to forgive her for living in sin with the 7th Earl of Cardigan. Adeline did this for a year before marrying him and, as if that wasn't bad enough in the 1850s, their affair was known to have begun whilst the Earl's first wife was still busy dying upstairs.

When they did marry, the Queen's response was to refuse to receive Adeline at Court, quite a snub for anyone, let alone the young wife of the hero of Balaclava. It clearly rankled too, for when Adeline married for a second time in 1873, this time to the Portuguese Don Antonio Manuel de Lancastere Soldana, Conde de Lancastre, she saw immediately that, by adapting her new title to its more English-sounding equivalent, she could have some small revenge on the Queen. (In 1909, the offence was further reinforced in her autobiography, *My Recollections* being credited to 'Adeline Louisa Maria de Horsey Cardigan and Lancaster' even though, strictly speaking, she was forbidden by the rules governing the British peerages to join her titles together in this way).

Perhaps as a result of her being barred from official entertainments, Adeline organised her own and rapidly became one of the unelected leaders of the so-called 'fast set' – a position she continued to hold into old age.

In later life, Adeline mostly divided her time between London and Deene Park, Northamptonshire – (the seat of the Cardigans, which she had somehow retained even after her remarriage – and continued to scandalise public opinion until well into old age by wearing particularly heavy make-up and organising steeplechases which were run through the middle of the local graveyard.

Soirées at Deene tended to follow a somewhat eccentric course too, with her Ladyship, on occasion, dressing up in flamenco gear to entertain her guests, something she was still doing when she was well into her 80s, and demanding that everyone pretend to faint when she appeared after dinner dressed as a nun. (Although she had long insisted that Deene Park was haunted by the ghost of a nun, this was apparently her idea of a joke rather than a genuine attempt to persuade people that the ghost was for real.)

Lady Lancastre also kept her own open coffin in the ballroom at Deene and, aided by her butler, would regularly climb in and out of it to reassure herself that it was still a good fit and comfortable enough to last her into the next world. Whenever she felt the need to do this, which was apparently rather often, the rest of the household would be required to attend and then afterwards be invited to give an opinion as to how her final send-off might be improved.

Unfortunately, although Adeline continued to live in the Earl's ancestral home following her marriage to the Portuguese count – Lord Cardigan had died after a fall from a horse, and as they had no children the title went to a cousin – she had access to the Cardigan fortune which soon collapsed under the weight of her extravagant lifestyle. Much of her distinctive apparel was then sold off when she was made bankrupt. As an old lady, however, she still attended the local meets in full hunting-dress, even though by this time it was her practice to arrive by coach, pretend to believe her groom had delivered her horse to the wrong place, and then settle down to observe the chase.

ALEXANDER, DUKE OF HAMILTON & BRANDON (1767-1852)

No so much feet of clay . . .

A man who collected titles as others collect stamps, Alexander Hamilton was not merely the 10th Duke of Hamilton and the 7th Duke of Brandon, but also a Marquis twice over – of Douglas and of Clydesdale – the Earl of Angus, Arran, Cambridge and Lanark, and the Baron of (deep breath) Abernathy, Jedburgh Forest, Polmont, Machanshire, Aven, Innerdale and Dutton. Little wonder, one might suppose, that his contemporaries described him as the proudest man of his day.

Hamilton was also known, perhaps a tad sarcastically, as *magnifico*, which is interesting because so was his near-contemporary John James Hamilton, Marquess of Abercorn (q.v.) with whom he quarrelled over the right to be known as the Duc de Chatelherault. In fact, Abercorn was right on that occasion, but this didn't prevent our man insisting that **he** was and adding the title to his own collection. (Later, he even had what he called the Chateau de Chatelherault built on his estate, as if to reinforce the false-hood). Nor was Hamilton prepared to let anything come between him and the Scottish throne, to which he insisted he was the heir by right of his descent from an earlier Earl of Arran, although, yet again, Abercorn's claim was by far the stronger.

Just like other English eccentrics, Hamilton also had the idea that a man of his stature needed a hermit around the place. He was unsuccessful in his quest too, even though, unlike the other hermit-seekers here described, the Duke was prepared to allow his to shave occasionally.

Hamilton's other quirks included a fascination with ancient Egyptian mummies and the techniques used to send their owners to the afterlife. He was sufficiently interested in this to retain the services of an acknowledged expert in the field, one Thomas Pettigrew, asking him to preserve his own body when the time came and to outbid the British Museum when a royal sarcophagus came up for sale.

In fact, His Grace paid the princely sum of £11,000 for this singular item before having it carted back from Thebes to Hamilton Palace, where-upon it was discovered that, having been constructed for an Egyptian princess, it was way too small for this particular Scottish nobleman. Unfortunately for the Duke, it was also carved from a stone which was too hard to allow for any modification to be made.

It would be nice to say that Hamilton lost no sleep over this but, in fact, he lost plenty and climbed into his precious box again and again, turning this way and that in an attempt to squeeze himself in. Perhaps to take his mind off it, Hamilton then turned his attention to the construction of the quite ridiculous Hamilton Mausoleum.

Here, the Duke found space beneath a 120-ft high dome for replicas of Ghiberti's Baptistery doors from Florence, an ornate octagonal family chapel, marble floors inlaid with many semi-precious stones, an array of statuary and, in its vast interior niches, room for his nine predecessors as well as any future heirs to the throne of Scotland.

'What a grand sight it will be, when Twelve Great Dukes of Hamilton rise together here at the Resurrection,' its creator was wont to tell visitors. In the event, of course, nothing of the sort happened and, in 1895, when there were at last 12 Dukes of Hamilton to rise up, the 12th of them, William Alexander Louis Stephen Douglas-Hamilton (who died in Algiers aged just 50) was recalled as exhibiting 'a frankness of speech bordering on rudeness' rather than as an appropriate guest to have at the Second Coming.

Ahead of this, the 10th Duke, having spent an estimated £130,000 on his Mausoleum, was still no closer to resolving the issue of how he was to fit into the sarcophagus. Indeed, his last words bore witness to his

preoccupation, 'Double me up! Double me up'. But sadly, this proved impossible, and, in the end his family took the decision to amputate his feet before having the eager Pettigrew go to work in accordance with his Grace's wishes.

It was a grim end for anyone, but at least the proudest man in Britain was spared one final ignominy when, after his death, the sarcophagus, upon being subjected to closer, more expert examination, was determined to be that of a minor court official rather than of a lady of royal blood . . .

LOONEY LAWS

- It is technically illegal for people in bath chairs to travel three abreast in London's Royal Parks. And, since a new law enacted as recently as 1977, members of the public are not allowed to touch a pelican 'without first having obtained written permission'.
- No such restrictions apply in Manchester and Birmingham, although it is an offence in both cities to fly a kite in the street or beat a carpet after eight o'clock in the morning.
- Despite the old Cockney song about rolling out the barrel, Londoners actually cannot do this along the city's pavements without the threat of a £20 fine.
- More bizarrely still, no-one living 'within a mile of an arsenal or explosive store', is allowed to possess a pack of cards.
- Back in London, one of two beadles or uniformed top-hatted watchmen is always on hand at the exclusive Burlington Arcade, just off Piccadilly, to prevent shoppers singing, whistling or opening an umbrella within the arcade. The rules were recently relaxed to enable them to carry their own shopping, however.
- Similarly, until as late as 1828, no non-royal was permitted to ride the length of Birdcage Walk in London. The only exceptions to this rule were the descendents of the first Duke of St Albans, the natural son of Charles II and Nell Gwyn.
- Members of Parliament enjoy numerous legal privileges when the Commons is in session, but they are still forbidden to attend the House wearing a full suit of armour, thanks to

an edict passed by Edward II in 1313 and never repealed.

- By contrast, anyone playing golf on Wimbledon Common can tee off wearing armour if it helps their game. In fact, they can wear whatever they like, providing it includes a pillar box-red outer garment – a requirement dating back to 1865 when Earl Spencer first gave leave to officers of the London Scottish Rifles to lay out a golf course on what was then his land.

- When not playing golf, all able-bodied Englishmen are, in theory, still required to practise their archery skills on a regular basis. This was Edward III's idea in 1349 and has never been rescinded. And in the ancient city of York, citizens are still permitted to shoot a Scotsman thanks to a local statute dating back to the days when cross-border hostilities were at their fiercest.

- Although the horsedrawn Hackney carriage is long gone, London cabbies are still required to carry 'sufficient foodstuffs for the horse'. Which is why the classic black cab was designed to provide space for a bale of straw next to the driver and with enough headroom to accommodate a man wearing a top hat. What's more, because the driver is not permitted to leave his or her cab on the public thoroughfare, official regulations require the call of nature to be answered 'against the rear of the vehicle, and in a seemly fashion' and for any passing police constable to shield the driver with his cape. . .

- Freemen of the City of London are still entitled to drive sheep across London's bridges, something last tested in 1999 by a 60 year-old from Muswell Hill who walked two sheep, Clover and Little Man, across Tower Bridge. The police objected and stopped him but, after investigating the matter further, had to let the eccentric threesome continue on its way.

- Her Majesty didn't insist on exercising her prerogative in 2006 when a young whale, apparently lost and confused, made its way up the Thames before dying. But the reigning monarch has, since the Middle Ages, been entitled to a share in any such animal, the head going to the king and the body to his queen (presumably to provide whalebone for her corsets).

- Fortunately, Her Majesty has also chosen not to exact the maximum penalty for anyone in the souvenir trade who uses her coat of arms without her permission. A law passed in 1592 calls for such miscreants to be beheaded and, for some reason, the crime of 'copying royal emblems' was exempted from the legislation to abolish capital punishment.
- Finally, butchers in London's Square Mile are theoretically still liable to spend a day in a pillory if they knowingly sell bad meat. This 600 year-old law also calls for them to suffer the further indignity of having the offending wares burnt beneath their noses.
- However, some of this stuff can occasionally work to your advantage. For example, if you fall foul of any law – loony or otherwise – you could do worse than run to Ely Place just off High Holborn in the City of London. The property of the Bishops of Ely since Medieval times, it's technically a part of Cambridgeshire not London. The entire street was thus off-limits to the Met. and, even now, police officers can reportedly enter it only if invited to do so.

Bibliography

Unless otherwise stated, all books are published in London

Axelrod, Alan: *International Encyclopaedia of Secret Societies and Fraternal Orders*, New York, Facts on File, 1997

Barker, Felix and Silvester-Carr, Denise: *The Black Plaque Guide to London*, Constable, 1987

Brabbs, Derry: *England's Heritage*, Cassell & Co., 2001

Briggs, Asa: *Victorian Things*, Penguin, 1988

Brook, Stephen: *The Club: The Jews of Modern Britain*, Constable, 1989

Burke, John: *Look Back on England*, Orbis, 1980

Cahill, Kevin: *Who Owns Britain*, Canongate, 2001

Cannadine, David: *Aspects of Aristocracy*, Yale, 1994. *The Decline and Fall of the British Aristocracy*, Yale, 1990. *The Pleasures of the Past*, Collins, 1989

Caufield, Catherine: *The Emperor of the United States of America and Other Magnificent British Eccentrics*, Routledge & Kegan Paul, 1981

Clark, Sir G (Ed.): *The Oxford History of England* (16 vols.), Oxford University Press, 1975

Clifton-Taylor, Alec: *Buildings of Delight*, Gollancz, 1988. *The Spirit of the Age*, British Broadcasting Corporation, 1975

Clunn, Harold P: *The Face of London*, Spring Books, 1957

David, Hugh: *Heroes, Mavericks and Bounders*, Michael Joseph, 1991

De'Ath, Richard: *Sod's Laws*, Robson Books, 1995

Dictionary of National Biography, Oxford University Press, 1975

Donaldson, William: *Brewer's Rogues, Villains & Eccentrics*, Cassell, 2002

Earl, Peter: *A City Full of People*, Methuen, 1994

English Heritage: *Blue Plaque Guide*, Journeyman Press, 1991

Fletcher, Geoffrey: *The London Nobody Knows*, Penguin, 1965

Fraser, Antonia: *King Charles II*, Weidenfeld & Nicolson, 1979

Gardiner, Julia (Ed.): *Who's Who in British History*, Collins & Brown, 2000

Gaunt, William: *Victorian Olympus*, Jonathan Cape, 1975

Graves, Charles: *Leather Armchairs*, Cassell, 1963

Greenwood, Douglas: *Who's Buried Where In England*, Constable, 1982

Halliday, Stephen: Newgate: *London's Prototype of Hell*, Sutton, 2006

Hart-Davis, Adam: *Eurekaaargh!*, Michael O'Mara, 1999

Headley, Gwyn and Meulencamp, Wim: *Follies*, Aurum, 1999

Hibbert, Christopher: *The Court of St James's*, Weidenfeld & Nicolson, 1979

– and Weinreb, Ben: *The London Encyclopaedia*, Macmillan, 1983

Jardine, Lisa: *Ingenious Pursuits*, Little, Brown, 1999

Jenkins, Simon: *City at Risk,* Hutchinson, 1970. *England's Thousand Best Houses*, Allen Lane, 2003

Kent, William: *An Encyclopaedia of London*, Dent, 1970

Kightly, Charles: *The Customs and Ceremonies of Britain*, Thames & Hudson, 1986

Lacey, Robert: *Aristocrats*, Hutchinson, 1983

Lees-Milne, James: *Earls of Creation*, Penguin, 2001

Long, David: *Spectacular Vernacular London's 100 Most Extraordinary Buildings*, History Press, Stroud, 2006. *Tunnels, Towers & Temples*, History Press, Stroud, 2007? *Little Book of London*, History Press Stroud, 2007. *Classic Cars*, Remember When, Barnsley, 2009

Lowe, Jacques & McLachlan, Sandy: *The City*, Quartet/Visual Arts, 1982

Lycett-Green, Candida: *England*: *Travels Through an Unwrecked Landscape*, Pavilion, 1996

Mace, Rodney: *Trafalgar Square: Emblem of Empire*, Lawrence & Wishart, 2005

Massingberd, Hugh: *Daily Telegraph Book of Obituaries*, (5 vols.), Macmillan, 1995–1999

Masters, Brian: *The Dukes*, Pimlico, 2001

Merullo, Annabel (Ed.): *British Greats*, Cassell, 2000

Michell, John: *Eccentric Lives & Peculiar Notions*, Thames & Hudson, 1984

Morgan, Chris & Langford, David: *Facts & Fallacies*, Webb & Bower, Exeter, 1981

Paxman, Jeremy: *The English*, Michael Joseph, 1998

Pearce, David: *The Great Houses of London*, Vendome Press, 1986

Pollins, Harold: *Economic History of the Jews in England*, Associated University Presses, 1982

Strong, Roy: *Lost Treasures of Britain*, Viking, 1990

Sykes, Christopher Simon: *Private Palaces*, Chatto & Windus, 1985

Timpson, John: *English Eccentrics*, Jarrold, Norwich, 1991

Trench, Richard and Hillman, Ellis: *London Under London*, John Murray, 1984

White, Colin: *The Trafalgar Captains*, Chatham Publishing, 2005

Willey, Russ: *London Gazetteer*, Chambers Harrap, Edinburgh, 2006

Index